GREAT JOBS

FOR

Computer Science Majors

Jan Goldberg

Revised by Mark Rowh

VGM Career Books

Chicago   New York   San Francisco   Lisbon   London   Madrid   Mexico City
Milan   New Delhi   San Juan   Seoul   Singapore   Sydney   Toronto

Library of Congress Cataloging-in-Publication Data

Goldberg, Jan.
    Great jobs for computer science majors / Jan Goldberg. — 2nd ed. / revised by Mark Rowh.
        p.   cm. — (Great jobs for)
    Includes index.
    ISBN 0-07-139039-1
    1. Computer science—Vocational guidance.   2. Computer industry—Employment.
    I. Rowh, Mark.   II. Title.   III. Series.

  QA76.25 .G62   2002
  004′.023—dc21   2002069133

1 2 3 4 5 6 7 8 9 0 LBM/LBM 1 0 9 8 7 6 5 4 3 2

ISBN 0-07-139039-1

McGraw-Hill books are available at special quantity discounts to use as premiums and sales promotions, or for use in corporate training programs. For more information, please write to the Director of Special Sales, Professional Publishing, McGraw-Hill, Two Penn Plaza, New York, NY 10121-2298. Or contact your local bookstore.

This book is printed on acid-free paper.

To my husband, Larry, for his continual love and support. To my daughters, Sherri and Debbi, for always believing in me. And to the memory of my father and mother, Sam and Sylvia Lefkovitz, for encouraging me to follow my dreams.

Contents

Introduction

Computer Science:
A Degree with Endless Possibilities

"Man is still the most extraordinary computer of all."
—JOHN F. KENNEDY

Is this the age of the computer? Maybe, but as powerful and flexible as computers can be, they are still merely tools. Without people, computers are not of much use.

From a career viewpoint, this is not a problem. In fact, the need for persons trained to work with computers in their many dimensions has continued to grow. Computers are integral to modern life, and new applications are introduced every day. As computers become more and more pervasive, the potential for computer-related careers continues to grow.

From Then to Now

Long before mechanical calculating devices were invented, astronomers, navigators, and scientists relied on books of tables for their calculations. These were completed by hand, typeset, and printed. Needless to say, calculations carried out by humans were subject to human error and the transcribing and typesetting produced additional errors. Thus, a new system had to be devised.

The seventeenth-century mathematicians Gottfried Wilhelm Leibniz and Blaise Pascal attacked this problem by developing mechanical calculators that could perform the basic mathematical functions of addition, subtraction, multiplication, and division and could do so with speed and fairly good accuracy. However, there were still problems with the creation and use of these devices, such as difficulties in building them. While some improvements were made from these early designs, in truth computing machinery didn't show much improvement for almost 200 years.

Englishman Charles Babbage authored a scientific paper in 1822 called "On the Theoretical Principles of the Machinery for Calculating Tables," which included a proposal to construct a machine called the Difference Engine designed to mechanize the production of tables. Later, Babbage changed his concept to an Analytical Engine that would be programmable. Babbage's ideas were well received by the Royal Astronomical Society, but circumstances prevented him from completing his project before his death in 1871. Though Babbage did not live to see it happen, he had a profound effect on computer technology. His use of punched cards as a storage device was 100 years ahead of its time, and the concepts of separate storage and computation units persist to this very day.

During the United States census of 1890, basic computing concepts evolved significantly. When the census had been done in 1880, it took eight years to process and tabulate the data. To speed up this process, Herman Hollerith built an electromechanical unit that processed information on punched cards. The inventor used the punched cards to record information such as age, sex, nationality, and other vital statistics. While punched cards are no longer used in connection with computers, parts of Hollerith's code are still used to instruct computers on how to read input and format output.

In the 1940s, the first fully electronic calculator to compute complex equations was constructed by J. Presper Eckert and John W. Mauchly. The unit did speed up the solving of complex mathematical problems but could not be programmed in the sense that we use that term today. Instead, it had to be rewired by hand to solve new problems. And when one of its almost 18,000 vacuum tubes failed (which happened quite often), the system could not work properly.

The 1948 development of the transistor by Bell Telephone Laboratories helped overcome this problem. With transistors, it was now possible to hand-wire basic operations into the computer itself, doing away with bulky and temperamental vacuum tubes and replacing them with smaller, more workable units.

Mathematician-scientist John Von Neumann made another important contribution with his concept of stored programs. This revolutionized the ease and speed with which a computer could be programmed; Von Neumann has been credited with defining the basic structure or design of the modern electronic digital computer.

Without the development of the semiconductor integrated circuit, however, the industry would undoubtedly have been confined to expensive specialized machines with only limited use.

In the 1950s, a process known as photolithography made it possible to print the wiring connecting circuit components much the same way that a photo can be printed from a negative. Distances between components were now greatly reduced. A few years later, researchers found a way to print the components themselves using a semiconductive material such as silicon. Now both wiring and components could be produced out of the same layer of semiconductive and other materials.

During the next couple of decades, the creation of increasingly powerful mainframe computers dominated the art and science of computing. But then in the 1970s and 1980s, a revolution occurred. The development and popularization of microcomputers—eventually known as personal computers—brought computing into homes, small businesses, offices, and virtually every type of organization. Then a dizzying array of developments made computing increasingly important for science, technology, commerce, and everyday personal life. The miniaturization of computer chips and other components, the creation of the Internet, the growth of E-mail, and the development of increasingly fast and powerful computers are just a few of these advancements.

In the twenty-first century, computers are no longer new on the scene. To the contrary, computers are everywhere. They are valued by society and, as a result, so are the computer scientists, systems analysts, software developers, and other specialists who work with them. For those who have elected to pursue training in computer science, information technology, or related areas, the future appears bright indeed.

Education Is Key

If you want to be competitive to prospective employers in the world of computers, it is very important to have a college degree—at least an undergraduate degree. This is the best way to ready yourself and to increase your chances in the job market. No matter what specific career you choose, a higher education will

1. Offer a broad base of knowledge and experiences
2. Allow you to increase and perfect your skills
3. Provide you with opportunities to gain important personal and professional contacts
4. Give you the knowledge you need to make an informed career decision

The job market can be intensely competitive. With a multitude of talented, dedicated people vying for each job opening, you must always seek to set yourself above and apart from the others. A dynamite combination is a college degree with at least one internship, additional formal training or study, and experience working in the field. That's the way to position yourself with an edge over other well-qualified candidates.

Remember, those with skills in computing are highly valued by employers. Be sure to take full advantage of your educational credentials.

PART ONE

THE JOB SEARCH

The Self-Assessment

Self-assessment is the process by which you begin to acknowledge your own particular blend of education, experiences, values, needs, and goals. It provides the foundation for career planning and the entire job search process. Self-assessment involves looking inward and asking yourself what can sometimes prove to be difficult questions. This self-examination should lead to an intimate understanding of your personal traits, your personal values, your consumption patterns and economic needs, your longer-term goals, your skill base, your preferred skills, and your underdeveloped skills.

You come to the self-assessment process knowing yourself well in some of these areas, but you may still be uncertain about other aspects. You may be well aware of your consumption patterns, but have you spent much time specifically identifying your longer-term goals or your personal values as they relate to work? No matter what level of self-assessment you have undertaken to date, it is now time to clarify all of these issues and questions as they relate to the job search.

The knowledge you gain in the self-assessment process will guide the rest of your job search. In this book, you will learn about all of the following tasks:

- Writing résumés
- Exploring possible job titles
- Identifying employment sites
- Networking
- Interviewing
- Following up
- Evaluating job offers

In each of these steps, you will rely on and often return to the understanding gained through your self-assessment. Any individual seeking employment must be able and willing to express these facets of his or her personality to recruiters and interviewers throughout the job search. This communication allows you to show the world who you are so that together with employers you can determine whether there will be a workable match with a given job or career path.

How to Conduct a Self-Assessment

The self-assessment process goes on naturally all the time. People ask you to clarify what you mean, you make a purchasing decision, or you begin a new relationship. You react to the world and the world reacts to you. How you understand these interactions and any changes you might make because of them are part of the natural process of self-discovery. There is, however, a more comprehensive and efficient way to approach self-assessment with regard to employment.

Because self-assessment can become a complex exercise, we have distilled it into a seven-step process that provides an effective basis for undertaking a job search. The seven steps include the following:

1. Understanding your personal traits
2. Identifying your personal values
3. Calculating your economic needs
4. Exploring your longer-term goals
5. Enumerating your skill base
6. Recognizing your preferred skills
7. Assessing skills needing further development

As you work through your self-assessment, you might want to create a worksheet similar to the one shown in Exhibit 1.1, starting on the following page. Or you might want to keep a journal of the thoughts you have as you undergo this process. There will be many opportunities to revise your self-assessment as you start down the path of seeking a career.

Step 1   Understanding Your Personal Traits
Each person has a unique personality that he or she brings to the job search process. Gaining a better understanding of your personal traits can help you evaluate job and career choices. Identifying these traits and then finding

Exhibit 1.1
SELF-ASSESSMENT WORKSHEET

Step 1. Understand Your Personal Traits

The personal traits that describe me are:
(Include all of the words that describe you.)
The ten personal traits that most accurately describe me are:
(List these ten traits.)

Step 2. Identify Your Personal Values

Working conditions that are important to me include:
(List working conditions that would have to exist for you to accept a position.)
The values that go along with my working conditions are:
(Write down the values that correspond to each working condition.)
Some additional values I've decided to include are:
(List those values you identify as you conduct this job search.)

Step 3. Calculate Your Economic Needs

My estimated minimum annual salary requirement is:
(Write the salary you have calculated based on your budget.)
Starting salaries for the positions I'm considering are:
(List the name of each job you are considering and the associated starting salary.)

Step 4. Explore Your Longer-Term Goals

My thoughts on longer-term goals right now are:
(Jot down some of your longer-term goals as you know them right now.)

Step 5. Enumerate Your Skill Base

The general skills I possess are:
(List the skills that underlie tasks you are able to complete.)
The specific skills I possess are:
(List more technical or specific skills that you possess, and indicate your level of expertise.)
General and specific skills that I want to promote to employers for the jobs I'm considering are:
(List general and specific skills for each type of job you are considering.)

continued

Step 6. Recognize Your Preferred Skills

Skills that I would like to use on the job include:

(List skills that you hope to use on the job, and indicate how often you'd like to use them.)

Step 7. Assess Skills Needing Further Development

Some skills that I'll need to acquire for the jobs I'm considering include:

(Write down skills listed in job advertisements or job descriptions that you don't currently possess.)

I believe I can build these skills by:

(Describe how you plan to acquire these skills.)

---

employment that allows you to draw on at least some of them can create a rewarding and fulfilling work experience. If potential employment doesn't allow you to use these preferred traits, it is important to decide whether you can find other ways to express them or whether you would be better off not considering this type of job. Interests and hobbies pursued outside of work hours can be one way to use personal traits you don't have an opportunity to draw on in your work. For example, if you consider yourself an outgoing person and the kinds of jobs you are examining allow little contact with other people, you may be able to achieve the level of interaction that is comfortable for you outside of your work setting. If such a compromise seems impractical or otherwise unsatisfactory, you probably should explore only jobs that provide the interaction you want and need on the job.

Many young adults who are not very confident about their attractiveness to employers will downplay their need for income. They will say, "Money is not all that important if I love my work." But if you begin to document exactly what you need for housing, transportation, insurance, clothing, food, and utilities, you will begin to understand that some jobs cannot meet your financial needs and it doesn't matter how wonderful the job is. If you have to worry each payday about bills and other financial obligations, you won't be very effective on the job. Begin now to be honest with yourself about your needs.

Inventorying Your Personal Traits. Begin the self-assessment process by creating an inventory of your personal traits. Using the list in Exhibit 1.2, decide which of these personal traits describe you.

Exhibit 1.2
PERSONAL TRAITS

Accurate	Eager	Inventive
Active	Easygoing	Jovial
Adaptable	Efficient	Just
Adventurous	Emotional	Kind
Affectionate	Empathetic	Liberal
Ambitious	Energetic	Likable
Analytical	Excitable	Logical
Appreciative	Expressive	Loyal
Artistic	Extroverted	Mature
Brave	Fair-minded	Methodical
Businesslike	Farsighted	Meticulous
Calm	Feeling	Mistrustful
Capable	Firm	Modest
Caring	Flexible	Motivated
Cautious	Formal	Objective
Cheerful	Friendly	Observant
Clean	Future-oriented	Open-minded
Competent	Generous	Opportunistic
Confident	Gentle	Optimistic
Conscientious	Good-natured	Organized
Conservative	Helpful	Original
Considerate	Honest	Outgoing
Cool	Humorous	Patient
Cooperative	Idealistic	Peaceful
Courageous	Imaginative	Personable
Creative	Impersonal	Persuasive
Critical	Independent	Pleasant
Curious	Individualistic	Poised
Daring	Industrious	Polite
Decisive	Informal	Practical
Deliberate	Innovative	Precise
Detail-oriented	Intellectual	Principled
Determined	Intelligent	Private
Discreet	Introverted	Productive
Dominant	Intuitive	Progressive

continued

Problem solver	Sedentary	Tactful
Quick	Self-confident	Thorough
Quiet	Self-controlled	Thoughtful
Rational	Self-disciplined	Tolerant
Realistic	Sensible	Trusting
Receptive	Serious	Trustworthy
Reflective	Sincere	Truthful
Relaxed	Sociable	Understanding
Reliable	Spontaneous	Unexcitable
Reserved	Strong	Uninhibited
Resourceful	Strong-minded	Verbal
Responsible	Structured	Versatile
Reverent	Subjective	Wise

Focusing on Selected Personal Traits. Of all the traits you identified from the list in Exhibit 1.2, select the ten you believe most accurately describe you. If you are having a difficult time deciding, think about which words people who know you well would use to describe you. Keep track of these ten traits.

Considering Your Personal Traits in the Job Search Process. As you begin exploring jobs and careers, watch for matches between your personal traits and the job descriptions you read. Some jobs will require many personal traits you know you possess, and others will not seem to match those traits.

> An information technology manager in a large corporation, for example, must interact with a range of personnel in various departments. He or she must have the ability to coordinate the schedules and activities of workers, an essential task for someone in this position. But a freelance software designer usually works alone, with limited opportunities to interact with others. Both often have deadlines to meet, but the software designer has far fewer people to answer to and must be able to work independently.

Your ability to respond to changing conditions, your decision-making ability, productivity, creativity, and verbal skills all have a bearing on your success in and enjoyment of your work life. To better guarantee success, be sure to take the time needed to understand these traits in yourself.

Step 2 Identifying Your Personal Values

Your personal values affect every aspect of your life, including employment, and they develop and change as you move through life. Values can be defined as principles that we hold in high regard, qualities that are important and desirable to us. Some values aren't ordinarily connected to work (love, beauty, color, light, relationships, family, or religion), and others are (autonomy, cooperation, effectiveness, achievement, knowledge, and security). Our values determine, in part, the level of satisfaction we feel in a particular job.

Defining Acceptable Working Conditions. One facet of employment is the set of working conditions that must exist for someone to consider taking a job.

Each of us would probably create a unique list of acceptable working conditions, but items that might be included on many people's lists are the amount of money you would need to be paid, how far you are willing to drive or travel, the amount of freedom you want in determining your own schedule, whether you would be working with people or data or things, and the types of tasks you would be willing to do. Your conditions might include statements of working conditions you will *not* accept; for example, you might not be willing to work at night or on weekends or holidays.

If you were offered a job tomorrow, what conditions would have to exist for you to realistically consider accepting the position? Take some time and make a list of these conditions.

Realizing Associated Values. Your list of working conditions can be used to create an inventory of your values relating to jobs and careers you are exploring. For example, if one of your conditions stated that you wanted to earn at least $30,000 per year, the associated value would be financial gain. If another condition was that you wanted to work with a friendly group of people, the value that went along with that might be belonging or interaction with people. Exhibit 1.3 provides a list of commonly held values that relate to the work environment; use it to create your own list of personal values.

Relating Your Values to the World of Work. As you read the job descriptions in this book and in other suggested resources, think about the values associated with each position.

Exhibit 1.3
WORK VALUES
_____

Achievement	Effectiveness	Precision
Advancement	Excitement	Prestige
Adventure	Fast pace	Privacy
Attainment	Financial gain	Profit
Authority	Helping	Recognition
Autonomy	Humor	Responsiblity
Belonging	Improvisation	Risk
Challenge	Independence	Security
Change	Influencing others	Self-expression
Communication	Intellectual stimulation	Solitude
Community	Interaction	Stability
Competition	Knowledge	Status
Completion	Leading	Structure
Contribution	Mastery	Supervision
Control	Mobility	Surroundings
Cooperation	Moral fulfillment	Teamwork
Creativity	Organization	Time freedom
Decision making	Physical activity	Variety
Development	Power	

In selling computer software, for instance, your duties may include calling on clients, explaining products and/or services you offer, arranging delivery, or providing follow-up services after the sale. Associated qualities include knowledge, mastery, competition, and variety.

If you were thinking about a career in this field, or any other field you're exploring, at least some of the associated values should match those you extracted from your list of working conditions. Take a second look at any values that don't match up. How important are they to you? What will happen if they are not satisfied on the job? Can you incorporate those personal values elsewhere? Your answers need to be brutally honest. As you continue your exploration, be sure to add to your list any additional values that occur to you.

Step 3 Calculating Your Economic Needs

Each of us grew up in an environment that provided for certain basic needs, such as food and shelter, and, to varying degrees, other needs that we now consider basic, such as cable television, E-mail, or an automobile. Needs such as privacy, space, and quiet, which at first glance may not appear to be monetary needs, may add to housing expenses and so should be considered as you examine your economic needs. For example, if you place a high value on a large, open living space for yourself, it would be difficult to satisfy that need without an associated high housing cost, especially in a densely populated city environment.

As you prepare to move into the world of work and become responsible for meeting your own basic needs, it is important to consider the salary you will need to be able to afford a satisfying standard of living. The three-step process outlined here will help you plan a budget, which in turn will allow you to evaluate the various career choices and geographic locations you are considering. The steps include (1) developing a realistic budget, (2) examining starting salaries, and (3) using a cost-of-living index.

Developing a Realistic Budget. Each of us has certain expectations for the kind of lifestyle we want to maintain. To begin the process of defining your economic needs, it will be helpful to determine what you expect to spend on routine monthly expenses. These expenses include housing, food, transportation, entertainment, utilities, loan repayments, and revolving charge accounts. A worksheet that details many of these expenses is shown in Exhibit 1.4. You may not currently spend anything for certain items, but you probably will have to once you begin supporting yourself. As you develop this budget, be generous in your estimates, but keep in mind any items that could be reduced or eliminated. If you are not sure about the cost of a certain item, talk with family or friends who would be able to give you a realistic estimate.

If this is new or difficult for you, start to keep a log of expenses right now. You may be surprised at how much you actually spend each month for food or stamps or magazines. Household expenses and personal grooming items can often loom very large in a budget, as can auto repairs or home maintenance.

Income taxes must also be taken into consideration when examining salary requirements. State and local taxes vary, so it is difficult to calculate exactly the effect of taxes on the amount of income you need to generate. To roughly estimate the gross income necessary to generate your minimum annual salary requirement, multiply the minimum salary you have calculated (see Exhibit 1.4) by a factor of 1.35. The resulting figure will be an approx-

Exhibit 1.4
ESTIMATED MONTHLY EXPENSES WORKSHEET

		Could Reduce Spending? (Yes/No)
Cable	$ _____	_____
Child care	_____	_____
Clothing	_____	_____
Educational loan repayment	_____	_____
Entertainment	_____	_____
Food		
At home	_____	_____
Meals out	_____	_____
Gifts	_____	_____
Housing		
Rent/mortgage	_____	_____
Insurance	_____	_____
Property taxes	_____	_____
Medical insurance	_____	_____
Reading materials	_____	_____
Newspapers	_____	_____
Magazines	_____	_____
Books	_____	_____
Revolving loans/charges	_____	_____
Savings	_____	_____
Telephone	_____	_____
Transportation		
Auto payment	_____	_____
Insurance	_____	_____
Parking	_____	_____
Gasoline	_____	_____
or		
Cab/train/bus fare	_____	_____
Utilities		
Electric	_____	_____
Gas	_____	_____
Water/sewer	_____	_____

	Could Reduce Spending? (Yes/No)	
Vacations		
Miscellaneous expense 1	_____	_____
Expense: _____		
Miscellaneous expense 2	_____	_____
Expense: _____		
Miscellaneous expense 3	_____	_____
Expense: _____		
TOTAL MONTHLY EXPENSES:	_____	_____
YEARLY EXPENSES		
(Monthly expenses × 12):	_____	_____
INCREASE TO INCLUDE TAXES		
(Yearly expenses × 1.35):	_____	_____ =
MINIMUM ANNUAL SALARY		
REQUIREMENT:	_____	

imation of what your gross income would need to be, given your estimated expenses.

Examining Starting Salaries. Starting salaries for each of the career tracks are provided throughout this book. These salary figures can be used in conjunction with the cost-of-living index (discussed in the next section) to determine whether you would be able to meet your basic economic needs in a given geographic location.

Using a Cost-of-Living Index. If you are thinking about trying to get a job in a geographic region other than the one where you now live, understanding differences in the cost of living will help you come to a more informed decision about making a move. By using a cost-of-living index, you can compare salaries offered and the cost of living in different locations with what you know about the salaries offered and the cost of living in your present location.

Many variables are used to calculate the cost-of-living index. Often included are housing, groceries, utilities, transportation, health care, clothing, and entertainment expenses. Right now you do not need to worry about the details associated with calculating a given index. The main purpose of this exercise is to help you understand that pay ranges for entry-level positions may not vary greatly, but the cost of living in different locations *can* vary tremendously.

If you lived in Atlanta, Georgia, for example, and you were interested in working as a systems analyst for a manufacturing firm, you would earn, on average, $49,000 annually. But let's say you're also thinking about moving to either Detroit, San Francisco, or Washington, D.C. You know you can live on $49,000 in Atlanta, but you want to be able to equate that salary in other locations you're considering. How much will you need to earn in those locations to do this? Figuring the cost of living for each city will show you.

Let's walk through this example. In any cost-of-living index, the number 100 represents the national average cost of living, and each city is assigned an index number based on current prices in that city for the items included in the index (housing, food, and so forth). In the index we used, Atlanta was assigned the number 102.8, Detroit's index was 109.3, San Francisco's was 118.9, and the index for Washington, D.C., was 129.3. In other words, it costs 25 percent more to live in Washington, D.C., than it does to live in Atlanta. We can

JOB: SYSTEMS ANALYST

City	Index	Equivalent Salary
Washington, D.C.	129.3	
		× $49,000 = $61,631 in Washington, D.C.
Atlanta	102.8	
San Francisco	118.9	
		× $49,000 = $56,674 in San Francisco
Atlanta	102.8	
Detroit	109.3	
		× $49,000 = $52,098 in Detroit
Atlanta	102.8	

set up a table to determine exactly how much you would have to earn in each of these cities to have the same buying power that you have in Atlanta.

You would have to earn $61,631 in Washington, D.C., $56,674 in San Francisco, and $52,098 in Detroit to match the buying power of $49,000 in Atlanta.

If you would like to determine whether it's financially worthwhile to make any of these moves, one more piece of information is needed: the U.S. Department of Labor reports the following average salary information for systems analyst for 2000:

Region	Annual Salary	Salary Equivalent to Georgia	Change in Buying Power
Middle Atlantic (including Washington, D.C.)	$69,638	$61,631	+$8,007
Pacific (including San Francisco)	$64,089	$56,674	+$7,410
East North Central (including Detroit)	$56,222	$52,098	+$4,124
East South Central (including Atlanta)	$49,504	—	—

Even with the greater cost of living, if you moved to Washington, D.C., and secured employment as a systems analyst you would be able to maintain a lifestyle similar to the one you led in Atlanta; in fact, you would have significant added income because of the higher salaries paid in that region. The same would also be true for a move to San Francisco or Detroit. You would increase your buying power given the rate of pay and cost of living in these cities.

You can work through a similar exercise for any type of job you are considering and for many locations when current salary information is available. It will be worth your time to undertake this analysis if you are seriously considering a relocation. By doing so you will be able to make an informed choice.

Step 4   Exploring Your Longer-Term Goals

There is no question that when we first begin working, our goals are to use our skills and education in a job that will reward us with employment, income, and status relative to the preparation we brought with us to this position. If we are not being paid as much as we feel we should for our level of education or if job demands don't provide the intellectual stimulation we had hoped for, we experience unhappiness and as a result often seek other employment.

Most jobs we consider "good" are those that fulfill our basic "lower-level" needs of security, food, clothing, shelter, income, and productive work. But even when our basic needs are met and our jobs are secure and productive, we as individuals are constantly changing. As we change, the demands and expectations we place on our jobs may change. Fortunately, some jobs grow and change with us, and this explains why some people are happy throughout many years in a job.

But more often people are bigger than the jobs they fill. We have more goals and needs than any job could satisfy. These are "higher-level" needs of self-esteem, companionship, affection, and an increasing desire to feel we are employing ourselves in the most effective way possible. Not all of these higher-level needs can be met through employment, but for as long as we are employed, we increasingly demand that our jobs play their part in moving us along the path to fulfillment.

Another obvious but important fact is that we change as we mature. Although our jobs also have the potential for change, they may not change as frequently or as markedly as we do. There are increasingly fewer one-job, one-employer careers; we must think about a work future that may involve voluntary or forced moves from employer to employer. Because of that very real possibility, we need to take advantage of the opportunities in each position we hold. Acquiring the skills and competencies associated with each position will keep us viable and attractive as employees. This is particularly true in a job market that not only is technology/computer dependent, but also is populated with more and more small, self-transforming organizations rather than the large, seemingly stable organizations of the past.

It may be difficult in the early stages of the job search to determine whether the path you are considering can meet these longer-term goals. Reading about career paths and individual career histories in your field can be very helpful in this regard. Meeting and talking with individuals further along in their careers can be enlightening as well. Older workers can provide valuable guidance on "self-managing" your career, which will become an increasingly valuable skill in the future. Some of these ideas may seem remote as you read this now, but you should be able to appreciate the need to ensure that you are growing, developing valuable new skills, and researching other employers who might be interested in your particular skills package.

If you are considering a position in software sales, talk to individuals who can provide an inside look at this area to gain a better perspective on this career. It would be worth your time to talk with an entry-level sales associate, a more experienced associate, and finally a vice president for sales who has a considerable work history in the sales area. Each will have a different perspective, unique concerns, and an individual set of value priorities.

Step 5 Enumerating Your Skill Base

In terms of the job search, skills can be thought of as capabilities that can be developed in school, at work, or by volunteering and then used in specific job settings. Many studies have documented the kinds of skills that employers seek in entry-level applicants. For example, some of the most desired skills for individuals interested in the teaching profession are the ability to interact effectively with students one-on-one, to manage a classroom, to adapt to varying situations as necessary, and to get involved in school activities. Business employers have also identified important qualities, including enthusiasm for the employer's product or service, a businesslike mind, the ability to follow written or oral instructions, the ability to demonstrate self-control, the confidence to suggest new ideas, the ability to communicate with all members of a group, an awareness of cultural differences, and loyalty, to name just a few. You will find that many of these skills are also in the repertoire of qualities demanded in your college major.

To be successful in obtaining any given job, you must be able to demonstrate that you possess a certain mix of skills that will allow you to carry out the duties required by that job. This skill mix will vary a great deal from job to job; to determine the skills necessary for the jobs you are seeking, you can read job advertisements or more generic job descriptions, such as those found later in this book. If you want to be effective in the job search, you must directly show employers that you possess the skills needed to be successful in filling the position. These skills will initially be described on your résumé and then discussed again during the interview process.

Skills are either general or specific. To develop a list of skills relevant to employers, you must first identify the general skills you possess, then list specific skills you have to offer, and, finally, examine which of these skills employers are seeking.

Identifying Your General Skills. Because you possess or will possess a college degree, employers will assume that you can read and write, perform certain basic computations, think critically, and communicate effectively. Employers will want to see that you have acquired these skills, and they will want to know which additional general skills you possess.

One way to begin identifying skills is to write an experiential diary. An experiential diary lists all the tasks you were responsible for completing for each job you've held and then outlines the skills required to do those tasks. You may list several skills for any given task. This diary allows you to distinguish between the tasks you performed and the underlying skills required to complete those tasks. Here's an example:

Tasks	Skills
Answering telephone	Effective use of language, clear diction, ability to direct inquiries, ability to solve problems
Waiting on tables	Poise under conditions of time and pressure, speed, accuracy, good memory, simultaneous completion of tasks, sales skills

For each job or experience you have participated in, develop a worksheet based on the example shown here. On a résumé, you may want to describe these skills rather than simply listing tasks. Skills are easier for the employer to appreciate, especially when your experience is very different from the employment you are seeking. In addition to helping you identify general skills, this experiential diary will prepare you to speak more effectively in an interview about the qualifications you possess.

Identifying Your Specific Skills. It may be easier to identify your specific skills because you can definitely say whether you can speak other languages, program a computer, draft a map or diagram, or edit a document using appropriate symbols and terminology.

Using your experiential diary, identify the points in your history where you learned how to do something very specific, and decide whether you have a beginning, intermediate, or advanced knowledge of how to use that particular skill. Right now, be sure to list *every* specific skill you have, and don't consider whether you like using the skill. Write down a list of specific skills you have acquired and the level of competence you possess—beginning, intermediate, or advanced.

Relating Your Skills to Employers. You probably have thought about a couple of different jobs you might be interested in obtaining, and one way to begin relating the general and specific skills you possess to a potential employer's needs is to read actual advertisements for these types of positions (see Part Two for resources listing actual job openings).

You might, for example, be interested in a career as a computer engineer. A typical job listing might read, "Requires 2–5 years experience, organizational and interpersonal skills, and the ability to work under pressure." If you then used any one of a number of general sources of information that describes the job of a computer engineer, you would find additional information. Computer engineers also work with the hardware and software aspects of system design and development. They may be involved with the design of new computing devices or computer-related equipment; they must be able to both work as part of a team and to function independently, depending on the job setting. And finally, they must also keep abreast of rapidly occurring advances in the field.

Start building a comprehensive list of required skills with the first job description you read. Explore advertisements for and descriptions of several types of related positions. This will reveal an important core of skills necessary for obtaining the type of work you're interested in. In building this list, include both general and specific skills.

Following is a sample list of skills needed to be successful as a computer engineer. These items were extracted from general resources and actual job listings.

JOB: COMPUTER ENGINEER

General Skills	Specific Skills
Gather information	Test computer designs
Have a specific body of knowledge	Be familiar with CASE tools
	Write memos

continued

General Skills	Specific Skills
Pay attention to detail	Be familiar with uses of virtual reality
Present technical knowledge in laymen's terms	Prepare specifications
Work well with other people	Create structural diagrams
Be organized	Write reports
Perform several tasks simultaneously	Be familiar with object-oriented programming languages
Be able to supervise the work of others	

Now, on separate sheets of paper, try to generate a comprehensive list of required skills for at least one job you are considering.

Any list of general skills that you develop for a given career path would be valuable for a number of jobs you might apply for. Many specific skills would also be transferable to other types of positions. For example, possessing expertise in Computer-Aided Software Engineering (CASE) would be a required skill for computer engineers, and it would also be a required skill for systems analysts.

Now review the list of skills that are required for jobs you are considering, and check off those skills that *you know you possess*. You should refer to these specific skills on the résumé that you write for this type of job. See Chapter 2 for details on résumé writing.

Step 6 Recognizing Your Preferred Skills

In the previous section you developed a comprehensive list of skills that relate to particular career paths that are of interest to you. You can now relate these to skills that you prefer to use. We all use a wide range of skills (some researchers say individuals have a repertoire of about five-hundred skills), but we may not particularly be interested in using all of them in our work. There may be some skills that come to us more naturally or that we use successfully time and time again and that we want to continue to use; these are best described as our preferred skills. For this exercise use the list of skills that you created for the previous section, and decide which of them you are *most interested in using* in future work and how often you would like to use them. You might be interested in using some skills only occasionally, while others you would like to use more regularly. You probably also have skills that you hope you can use constantly.

As you examine job announcements, look for matches between this list of preferred skills and the qualifications described in the advertisements. These skills should be highlighted on your résumé and discussed in job interviews.

Step 7 Assessing Skills Needing Further Development

Previously you compiled a list of general and specific skills required for given positions. You already possess some of these skills; those that remain to be developed are your underdeveloped skills.

If you are just beginning the job search, there may be gaps between the qualifications required for some of the jobs you're considering and skills you possess. The thought of having to admit to and talk about these under-developed skills, especially in a job interview, is a frightening one. One way to put a healthy perspective on this subject is to target and relate your exploration of underdeveloped skills to the types of positions you are seeking. Recognizing these shortcomings and planning to overcome them with either on-the-job training or additional formal education can be a positive way to address the concept of underdeveloped skills.

On your worksheet or in your journal, make a list of up to five general or specific skills required for the positions you're interested in that you *don't currently possess*. For each item list an idea you have for specific action you could take to acquire that skill. Do some brainstorming to come up with possible actions. If you have a hard time generating ideas, talk to people currently working in this type of position, professionals in your college career services office, trusted friends, family members, or members of related professional associations.

If, for example, you are interested in a job for which you don't have some specific required experience, you could locate training opportunities such as classes or workshops offered through a local college or university, community college, or club or association that would help you build the level of expertise you need for the job.

You will notice in this book that many excellent positions for your major demand computer skills. While basic word processing has been something you've done all through college, you may be surprised at the additional computer skills required by employers. Many positions for college graduates will ask for some familiarity with spreadsheet programming, and frequently some database-management software familiarity is a job demand as well. Desktop publishing software, graphics programs, and basic Web-page design also pop up frequently in job ads for college graduates. If your degree program hasn't introduced you to a wide variety of computer applications, what are your options? If you're still in college, take what computer courses you can before you graduate. If you've already graduated, look at evening programs, continuing education courses, or tutorial programs that may be available commercially. Developing a modest level of expertise will encourage you to be more confident in suggesting to potential employers that you can continue to add to your skill base on the job.

In Chapter 5 on interviewing, we will discuss in detail how to effectively address questions about underdeveloped skills. Generally speaking, though, employers want genuine answers to these types of questions. They want you to reveal "the real you," and they also want to see how you answer difficult questions. In taking the positive, targeted approach discussed above, you show the employer that you are willing to continue to learn and that you have a plan for strengthening your job qualifications.

Using Your Self-Assessment

Exploring entry-level career options can be an exciting experience if you have good resources available and will take the time to use them. Can you effectively complete the following tasks?

1. Understand your personality traits and relate them to career choices
2. Define your personal values
3. Determine your economic needs
4. Explore longer-term goals
5. Understand your skill base
6. Recognize your preferred skills
7. Express a willingness to improve on your underdeveloped skills

If so, then you can more meaningfully participate in the job search process by writing a more effective résumé, finding job titles that represent work you are interested in doing, locating job sites that will provide the opportunity for you to use your strengths and skills, networking in an informed way, participating in focused interviews, getting the most out of follow-up contacts, and evaluating job offers to find those that create a good match between you and the employer. The remaining chapters in Part One guide you through these next steps in the job search process. For many job seekers, this process can take anywhere from three months to a year to implement. The time you will need to put into your job search will depend on the type of job you want and the geographic location where you'd like to work. Think of your effort as a job in itself, requiring you to set aside time each week to complete the needed work. Carefully undertaken efforts may reduce the time you need for your job search.

2

The Résumé and Cover Letter

The task of writing a résumé may seem overwhelming if you are unfamiliar with this type of document, but there are some easily understood techniques that can and should be used. This section was written to help you understand the purpose of the résumé, the different types of résumé formats available, and how to write the sections of information traditionally found on a résumé. We will present examples and explanations that address questions frequently posed by people writing their first résumé or updating an old résumé.

Even within the formats and suggestions given, however, there are infinite variations. True, most résumés follow one of the outlines suggested, but you should feel free to adjust the résumé to suit your needs and make it expressive of your life and experience.

Why Write a Résumé?

The purpose of a résumé is to convince an employer that you should be interviewed. Whether you're mailing, faxing, or E-mailing this document, you'll want to present enough information to show that you can make an immediate and valuable contribution to an organization. A résumé is not an in-depth historical or legal document; later in the job search process you may be asked to document your entire work history on an application form and attest to its validity. The résumé should, instead, highlight relevant information pertaining directly to the organization that will receive the document or to the type of position you are seeking.

We will discuss four types of résumés in this chapter: chronological, functional, targeted, and digital. The reasons for using one type of résumé over another and the typical format for each are addressed in the following sections.

The Chronological Résumé

The chronological résumé is the most common of the various résumé formats and therefore the format that employers are most used to receiving. This type of résumé is easy to read and understand because it details the chronological progression of jobs you have held. (See Exhibit 2.1.) It begins with your most recent employment and works back in time. If you have a solid work history or have experience that provided growth and development in your duties and responsibilities, a chronological résumé will highlight these achievements. The typical elements of a chronological résumé include the heading, a career objective, educational background, employment experience, activities, and references.

The Heading

The heading consists of your name, address, telephone number, and other means of contact. This may include a fax number, E-mail address, and your home-page address. If you are using a shared E-mail account or a parent's business fax, be sure to let others who use these systems know that you may receive important professional correspondence via these systems. You wouldn't want to miss a vital E-mail or fax! Likewise, if your résumé directs readers to a personal home page on the Web, be certain it's a professional personal home page designed to be viewed and appreciated by a prospective employer. This may mean making substantial changes in the home page you currently mount on the Web.

We suggest that you spell out your full name in your résumé heading and type it in all capital letters in bold type. After all, you are the focus of the résumé! If you have a current as well as a permanent address and you include both in the heading, be sure to indicate until what date your current address will be valid. The two-letter state abbreviation should be the only abbreviation that appears in your heading. Don't forget to include the zip code with your address and the area code with your telephone number.

The Objective

As you formulate the wording for this part of your résumé, keep the following points in mind.

Exhibit 2.1
CHRONOLOGICAL RÉSUMÉ

PAUL JUAREZ

Linton Hall #346
University of California
Santa Cruz, CA 95060
(408) 555-2331
(until September 2002)

3220 Sebastian
Montreal, P.Q.
H3H 1H9
Canada
(514) 555-4550

OBJECTIVE

A career as a computer games software designer for a major manufacturer, ultimately moving into management.

EDUCATION

Bachelor of Science in Computer Science
University of California
Santa Cruz, California
September 2002

RELATED COURSES

Database Management   Research Design
Business Systems Design   Personnel Management
Real Estate Investment   Labor Relations

EXPERIENCE

Self-Employed
Designed and self-marketed *Vaders*, computer action game
2001 to present

Internship
Computer Support Analyst
America Online
Provided technical assistance to America Online members; worked with other technicians and AOL full-time staff to troubleshoot system problems
2000 to Present

continued

Part-Time/Summers
Computer Sales
CompUSA, Santa Cruz, California
Direct floor sales, providing assistance to customers and answering questions related to various hardware and software
1999 to 2001

PORTFOLIO
Portfolio of my computer games completed during the last two years is available upon request.

REFERENCES
Both personal and professional references are available upon request.

The Objective Focuses the Résumé. Without a doubt this is the most challenging part of the résumé for most writers. Even for individuals who have decided on a career path, it can be difficult to encapsulate all they want to say in one or two brief sentences. For job seekers who are unfocused or unclear about their intentions, trying to write this section can inhibit the entire résumé writing process.

Recruiters tell us time and time again that the objective creates a frame of reference for them. It helps them see how you express your goals and career focus. In addition, the statement may indicate in what ways you can immediately benefit an organization. Given the importance of the objective, every point covered in the résumé should relate to it. If information doesn't relate, it should be omitted. You'll file a number of résumé variations in your computer. There's no excuse for not being able to tailor a résumé to individual employers or specific positions.

Choose an Appropriate Length. Because of the brevity necessary for a résumé, you should keep the objective as short as possible. Although objectives of only four or five words often don't show much direction, objectives that take three full lines could be viewed as too wordy and might possibly be ignored.

Consider Which Type of Objective Statement You Will Use. There are many ways to state an objective, but generally there are four forms this statement can take: (1) a very general statement; (2) a statement focused on a specific position; (3) a statement focused on a specific industry; or (4) a summary of your qualifications. In our contacts with employers, we often hear that many résumés don't exhibit any direction or career goals, so we suggest avoiding general statements when possible.

1. General Objective Statement. General objective statements look like the following:

- An entry-level educational programming coordinator position
- An entry-level marketing position

This type of objective would be useful if you know what type of job you want but you're not sure which industries interest you.

2. Position-Focused Objective. Following are examples of objectives focusing on a specific position:

- To obtain the position of conference coordinator at State College
- To obtain a position as assistant editor at *Time* magazine

When a student applies for an advertised job opening, this type of focus can be very effective. The employer knows that the applicant has taken the time to tailor the résumé specifically for this position.

3. Industry-Focused Objective. Focusing on a particular industry in an objective could be stated as follows:

- To begin a career as an applications engineer in the biomedical device industry

4. Summary of Qualifications Statement. The summary of qualifications can be used instead of an objective or in conjunction with an objective. The purpose of this type of statement is to highlight relevant qualifications gained through a variety of experiences. This type of statement is often used by individuals with extensive and diversified work experience. An example of a qualifications statement follows:

A bachelor's degree in computer science and two years of progressively increasing responsibilities in the financial department of a national bank as an applications programmer have prepared me for a career in an organization that values hands-on involvement and thoroughness.

___

Support Your Objective. A résumé that contains any one of these types of objective statements should then go on to demonstrate why you are qualified to get the position. Listing academic degrees can be one way to indicate qualifications. Another demonstration would be in the way previous experiences, both volunteer and paid, are described. Without this kind of documentation in the body of the résumé, the objective looks unsupported. Think of the résumé as telling a connected story about you. All the elements should work together to form a coherent picture that ideally should relate to your statement of objective.

Education

This section of your résumé should indicate the exact name of the degree you will receive or have received, spelled out completely with no abbreviations. The degree is generally listed after the objective, followed by the institution name and location, and then the month and year of graduation. This section could also include your academic minor, grade point average (GPA), and appearance on the Dean's List or President's List.

If you have enough space, you might want to include a section listing courses related to the field in which you are seeking work. The best use of a "related courses" section would be to list some course work that is not traditionally associated with the major. Perhaps you took several computer courses outside your degree that will be helpful and related to the job prospects you are entertaining. Several education section examples are shown here:

___

- Bachelor of Science degree in Computer Science
  Northeastern University, Boston, Massachusetts,
  May 2002
  Minor: Accounting
- Bachelor of Science degree in Computer Science
  Tufts University, Medford, Massachusetts,
  December 2002
  Minor: Mathematics

- Bachelor of Science degree in Computer Science
  State University, Boulder, Colorado, December 2002
  Minor: Statistics

An example of a format for a related courses section follows:

Database Administration	Urban Planning
Business Computer Applications	Economics
Business Research Design	Actuary Science

Experience

The experience section of your résumé should be the most substantial part and should take up most of the space on the page. Employers want to see what kind of work history you have. They will look at your range of experiences, longevity in jobs, and specific tasks you are able to complete. This section may also be called "work experience," "related experience," "employment history," or "employment." No matter what you call this section, some important points to remember are the following:

1. **Describe your duties** as they relate to the position you are seeking.
2. **Emphasize major responsibilities** and indicate increases in responsibility. Include all relevant employment experiences: summer, part-time, internships, cooperative education, or self-employment.
3. **Emphasize skills**, especially those that transfer from one situation to another. The fact that you coordinated a student organization, chaired meetings, supervised others, and managed a budget leads one to suspect that you could coordinate other things as well.
4. **Use descriptive job titles** that provide information about what you did. A "Student Intern" should be more specifically stated as, for example, "Civil Engineering Intern." "Volunteer" is also too general; a title such as "Peer Writing Tutor" would be more appropriate.
5. **Create word pictures** by using active verbs to start sentences. Describe *results* you have produced in the work you have done.

A limp description would say something such as the following: "My duties included helping with production, proofreading, and editing. I used a design

Exhibit 2.2
RÉSUMÉ ACTION VERBS

Achieved	Eliminated	Monitored
Acted	Ensured	Negotiated
Administered	Established	Observed
Advised	Estimated	Obtained
Analyzed	Evaluated	Operated
Assessed	Examined	Organized
Assisted	Explained	Participated
Attained	Facilitated	Performed
Balanced	Finalized	Planned
Budgeted	Generated	Predicted
Calculated	Handled	Prepared
Collected	Headed	Presented
Communicated	Helped	Processed
Compiled	Identified	Produced
Completed	Illustrated	Projected
Composed	Implemented	Proposed
Conceptualized	Improved	Provided
Condensed	Increased	Qualified
Conducted	Influenced	Quantified
Consolidated	Informed	Questioned
Constructed	Initiated	Realized
Controlled	Innovated	Received
Converted	Instituted	Recommended
Coordinated	Instructed	Recorded
Corrected	Integrated	Reduced
Created	Interpreted	Reinforced
Decreased	Introduced	Reported
Defined	Learned	Represented
Demonstrated	Lectured	Researched
Designed	Led	Resolved
Determined	Maintained	Reviewed
Developed	Managed	Scheduled
Directed	Mapped	Selected
Documented	Marketed	Served
Drafted	Met	Showed
Edited	Modified	Simplified

Sketched	Studied	Tested
Sold	Submitted	Transacted
Solved	Summarized	Updated
Staffed	Systematized	Verified
Streamlined	Tabulated	

and page layout program." An action statement would be stated as follows: "Coordinated and assisted in the creative marketing of brochures and seminar promotions, becoming proficient in Quark."

Remember, an accomplishment is simply a result, a final measurable product that people can relate to. A duty is not a result; it is an obligation—every job holder has duties. For an effective résumé, list as many results as you can. To make the most of the limited space you have and to give your description impact, carefully select appropriate and accurate descriptors from the list of action words in Exhibit 2.2.

Here are some traits that employers tell us they like to see:

- Teamwork
- Energy and motivation
- Learning and using new skills
- Versatility
- Critical thinking
- Understanding how profits are created
- Organizational acumen
- Communicating directly and clearly, in both writing and speaking
- Risk taking
- Willingness to admit mistakes
- High personal standards

Solutions to Frequently Encountered Problems

Repetitive Employment with the Same Employer

EMPLOYMENT: The Foot Locker, Portland, Oregon. Summer 2001, 2002, 2003. Initially employed in high school as salesclerk. Due to successful performance, asked to return next two summers at higher pay with added responsibility. Ranked as the #2 salesperson the first summer and #1 the next two summers. Assisted in arranging eye-catching retail displays; served as manager of other summer workers during owner's absence.

A Large Number of Jobs

EMPLOYMENT: Recent Hospitality Industry Experience: Affiliated with four upscale hotel/restaurant complexes (September 2001–February 2004), where I worked part- and full-time as a waiter, bartender, disc jockey, and bookkeeper to produce income for college.

Several Positions with the Same Employer

EMPLOYMENT: Coca-Cola Bottling Co., Burlington, Vermont, 2001–2004. In four years, I received three promotions, each with increased pay and responsibility.

Summer Sales Coordinator: Promoted to hire, train, and direct efforts of add-on staff of fifteen college-age route salespeople hired to meet summer peak demand for product.

Sales Administrator: Promoted to run home office sales desk, managing accounts and associated delivery schedules for professional sales force of ten people. Intensive phone work, daily interaction with all personnel, and strong knowledge of product line required.

Route Salesperson: Summer employment to travel and tourism industry sites that use Coke products. Met specific schedule demands, used good communication skills with wide variety of customers, and demonstrated strong selling skills. Named salesperson of the month for July and August of that year.

Questions Résumé Writers Often Ask

How Far Back Should I Go in Terms of Listing Past Jobs?

Usually, listing three or four jobs should suffice. If you did something back in high school that has a bearing on your future aspirations for employment, by all means list the job. As you progress through your college career, high school jobs will be replaced on the résumé by college employment.

Should I Differentiate Between Paid and Nonpaid Employment?

Most employers are not initially concerned about how much you were paid. They are anxious to know how much responsibility you held in your past employment. There is no need to specify that your work was as a volunteer if you had significant responsibilities.

How Should I Represent My Accomplishments or Work-Related Responsibilities?

Succinctly, but fully. In other words, give the employer enough information to arouse curiosity but not so much detail that you leave nothing to the imagination. Besides, some jobs merit more lengthy explanations than others. Be sure to convey any information that can give an employer a better understanding of the depth of your involvement at work. Did you supervise others? How many? Did your efforts result in a more efficient operation? How much did you increase efficiency? Did you handle a budget? How much? Were you promoted in a short time? Did you work two jobs at once or fifteen hours per week after high school? Where appropriate, quantify.

Should the Work Section Always Follow the Education Section on the Résumé?

Always lead with your strengths. If your education closely relates to the employment you now seek, put this section after the objective. If your education does not closely relate but you have a surplus of good work experiences, consider reversing the order of your sections to lead with employment, followed by education.

How Should I Present My Activities, Honors, Awards, Professional Societies, and Affiliations?

This section of the résumé can add valuable information for an employer to consider if used correctly. The rule of thumb for information in this section is to include only those activities that are in some way relevant to the objective stated on your résumé. If you can draw a valid connection between your activities and your objective, include them; if not, leave them out.

Granted, this is hard to do. Playing center on the championship basketball team or serving as coordinator of the biggest homecoming parade ever held are roles that have meaning for you and represent personal accomplishments you'd like to share. But the résumé is a brief document, and the information you provide on it should help the employer make a decision about your job eligibility. Including personal details can be confusing and could hurt your candidacy. Limiting your activity list to a few significant experiences can be very effective.

If you are applying for a position as a safety officer, your certificate in Red Cross lifesaving skills or CPR would be related and valuable. You would want to include it. If, however, you are applying for a job as a junior account executive in an advertising agency, that information would be unrelated and superfluous. Leave it out.

Professional affiliations and honors should all be listed; especially important are those related to your job objective. Social clubs and activities need not be a part of your résumé unless you hold a significant office or you are looking for a position related to your membership. Be aware that most prospective employers' principal concerns are related to your employability, not your social life. If you have any, publications can be included as an addendum to your résumé.

The focus of the résumé is your experience and education. It is not necessary to describe your involvement in activities. However, if your résumé needs to be lengthened, this section provides the freedom either to expand on or mention only briefly the contributions you have made. If you have made significant contributions (e.g., an officer of an organization or a particularly long tenure with a group), you may choose to describe them in more detail. It is not always necessary to include the dates of your memberships with your activities the way you would include job dates.

There are various ways in which to present additional information. You may give this section a number of different titles. Assess what you want to list, and then use an appropriate title. Do not use "extracurricular activities." This terminology is scholastic, not professional, and therefore not appropriate. The following are two examples:

- ACTIVITIES: Society for Technical Communication, Student Senate, Student Admissions Representative, Senior Class Officer

- ACTIVITIES:
  - Society for Technical Communication Member
  - Student Senator
  - Student Admissions Representative
  - Senior Class Officer

The position you are looking for will determine what you should or should not include. Always look for a correlation between the activity and the prospective job.

How Should I Handle References?

The use of references is considered a part of the interview process, and they should never be listed on a résumé. You would always provide references to a potential employer if requested to, so it is not even necessary to include this section on the résumé if space does not permit. If space is available, it is acceptable to include one of the following statements:

- REFERENCES: Furnished upon request.
- REFERENCES: Available upon request.

Individuals used as references must be protected from unnecessary contacts. By including names on your résumé, you leave your references unprotected. Overuse and abuse of your references will lead to less-than-supportive comments. Protect your references by giving out their names only when you are being considered seriously as a candidate for a given position.

The Functional Résumé

The functional résumé departs from a chronological résumé in that it organizes information by specific accomplishments in various settings: previous jobs, volunteer work, associations, and so forth. This type of résumé permits you to stress the substance of your experiences rather than the position titles you have held. (See Exhibit 2.3.) You should consider using a functional résumé if you have held a series of similar jobs that relied on the same skills or abilities.

The Objective
A functional résumé begins with an objective that can be used to focus the contents of the résumé.

Specific Accomplishments
Specific accomplishments are listed on this type of résumé. Examples of the types of headings used to describe these capabilities might include research, computer skills, teaching, communication, production, management, marketing, or writing. The headings you choose will directly relate to your experience and the tasks that you carried out. Each accomplishment section contains statements related to your experience in that category, regardless of when or where it occurred. Organize the accomplishments and the related tasks you describe in their order of importance as related to the position you seek.

Experience or Employment History
Your actual work experience is condensed and placed after the specific accomplishments section. It simply lists dates of employment, position titles, and employer names.

Exhibit 2.3
FUNCTIONAL RÉSUMÉ

ELIZABETH JOHNSON

Lawrence Hall, Room 234
University of Florida
Gainesville, FL 34233
(904) 555-2146
ejohn@xxx.com

4020 Bay Road
Delray Beach, FL 33446
(561) 555-9943

OBJECTIVE

A position as a systems analyst for a major institution that will allow me to build upon my past experience and use my problem-solving skills.

CAPABILITIES

- Analytical problem solver
- Experienced systems analyst
- Experienced with library information systems
- Effective communicator
- Strong people skills

SELECTED ACCOMPLISHMENTS

Systems Analysis—Through a college work-study program I achieved three years of progressively more challenging duties in the library at the University of Florida in Gainesville. I helped design and implement a new system for cataloging and retrieving periodicals and instructed library staff in its use. Worked with mainframe and PC hardware and a variety of software.

Problem Solving—I worked in the university's admissions office, debugging a program to keep track of new student applications.

Team Player—Collaborated with coworkers and professionals in other university departments including the registrar's office and two other libraries on campus.

AWARDS

Dean's List (7 semesters)

EMPLOYMENT HISTORY

Hayes Library, University of Florida, Gainesville, 1994–present
Admissions Office, University of Florida, Gainesville, 1993–1995

EDUCATION
Bachelor of Science
Computer Information Systems
University of Florida
Gainesville, Florida
June 2002

REFERENCES
Provided upon request.

Education

The education section of a functional résumé is identical to that of the chronological résumé, but it does not carry the same visual importance because it is placed near the bottom of the page.

References

Because actual reference names are never listed on a résumé, a statement of reference availability is optional.

The Targeted Résumé

The targeted résumé focuses on specific work-related capabilities you can bring to a given position within an organization. (See Exhibit 2.4.) It should be sent to an individual within the organization who makes hiring decisions about the position you are seeking.

The Objective

The objective on this type of résumé should be targeted to a specific career or position. It should be supported by the capabilities, accomplishments, and achievements documented in the résumé.

Capabilities

Capabilities should be statements that illustrate tasks you believe you are capable of based on your accomplishments, achievements, and work history. Each should relate to your targeted career or position. You can stress your qualifications rather than your employment history. This approach may require research to obtain an understanding of the nature of the work involved and the capabilities necessary to carry out that work.

Exhibit 2.4
TARGETED RÉSUMÉ

THOMAS R. BERNADINO

Lindsley Hall #450
University of Wisconsin
Madison, WI 53706
(608) 555-2478
(until June 2002)

878 Marion Street
Glenview, IL 60025
(847) 555-0980

JOB TARGET
CAD Specialist with an architectural design firm

CAPABILITIES
- Familiarity with a variety of CAD software
- Organizational skills
- Excellent communicator, both written and oral
- Proven team skills
- Bilingual, Spanish and English

ACHIEVEMENTS
- Several articles published in local newspapers
- Designed brochures and logos for campus student activity groups
- Worked on design of community Victory Garden project
- Maintained a 4.0 average throughout college

WORK HISTORY

2001–present　Student Internship
Birch and Caplan Architectural Firm
Madison, WI
- Assisted several architects and draftsmen with a variety of projects including a new office building complex

1998–2001　Work-Study Position
Yearbook Office
University of Wisconsin, Madison, WI
- Using CAD software, designed the layout for three yearbooks

---

1998–2000	Summer Position (two summers)
	Hahnaman Hospital, Chicago, IL
	• Orderly for the pediatric unit. Performed a variety of duties following the directions of the nursing staff, including escorting patients to x-ray and the OR

EDUCATION
June 2002
Bachelor of Arts, Graphic Arts
University of Wisconsin, Madison, WI

Accomplishments/Achievements
This section relates the various activities you have been involved in to the job market. These experiences may include previous jobs, extracurricular activities at school, internships, and part-time summer work.

Experience
Your work history should be listed in abbreviated form and may include position title, employer name, and employment dates.

Education
Because this type of résumé is directed toward a specific job target and an individual's related experience, the education section is not prominently located at the top of the résumé as is done on the chronological résumé.

Digital Résumés

Today's employers have to manage an enormous number of résumés. One of the most frequent complaints the writers of this series hear from students is the failure of employers to even acknowledge the receipt of a résumé and cover letter. Frequently, the reason for this poor response or nonresponse is the volume of applications received for every job. In an attempt to better manage the considerable labor investment involved in processing large numbers of résumés, many employers are requiring digital submission of résumés. (See Exhibit 2.5.) There are two types of digital résumés: those that can be E-mailed or posted to a website, called *electronic résumés*, and those that can

Exhibit 2.5
DIGITAL RÉSUMÉ

JASON A. COLLINS
4322 Bank Street
Raleigh, NC 27695
(919) 555-2449
Cell: 555/123-4567
jcoll22@xxx.net

KEYWORD SUMMARY
B.S. Computer Applications, 2002
Network Management, Computer Applications
Database Management, Microsoft Certified

EDUCATION
B.S., Computer Applications, 2002
Concentration: Networking
North Carolina State University

M.S. in progress (part-time), North Carolina
    State University

HONORS
Tau Kappa Phi Computer Honor Society
Who's Who in Colleges and Universities
Honor Roll Eight Semesters

SKILLS
Computer hardware: PC and Macintosh computers
Network configuration
Various types of software and programming languages
Microsoft Certification

FOREIGN LANGUAGES
Fluent in Spanish
Study Abroad: Madrid, Spain 2000

WORK EXPERIENCE
2002–Present   Assistant Network Director, TriStem Incorporated
                   Raleigh, North Carolina
                   * Assist in day to day operation of company's computer
                     network

Put your name at the top on its own line.

Put your phone number on its own line.

Use a standard-width typeface.

Keywords make your résumé easier to find in a database.

Capital letters emphasize headings.

No line should exceed sixty-five characters.

End each line by hitting the enter key.

```
                    * Support comprehensive data base      Use a space between
                    * Assist in equipment acquisition,      asterisk and text
                      installation and maintenance
                    * Assist in software acquisition and
                      integration
                    * Provide training for users
                    * Perform other related duties
   2000–2002        Network Technician, Montgomery Area Hospital
                    Burlington, North Carolina
                    * Installed and maintained equipment
                    * Performed network management responsibilities under
                      direction of network director.
   1998–2000        Math Tutor, North Carolina State University
                    Also ran home-based computer repair business on part-time
                    basis
```

ACTIVITIES

Vice President, Computer Applications Society, 2001
Senator, Student Government, 1999–2001
Volunteer, Habitat for Humanity, Summer 1998–present

SPECIAL SKILLS

* Skilled in all aspects of developing and coordinating a local area network
* Knowledgeable of wide area networks and other networking arrangements
* Up-to-date in hardware developments
* Skilled in using various software packages
* Flexible and persistent in trouble-shooting, problem-solving and continuous
  improvement efforts

REFERENCES

Available on request.

---

be "read" by a computer, commonly called *scannable résumés*. Though the format may be a bit different from the traditional "paper" résumé, the goal of both types of digital résumés is the same—to get you an interview! These résumés must be designed to be "technologically friendly." What that basically means to you is that they should be free of graphics and fancy formatting.

Electronic Résumés

Sometimes referred to as plain-text résumés, electronic résumés are designed to be E-mailed to an employer or posted to one of many commercial Internet databases such as CareerMosaic.com, America's Job Bank (ajb.dni.us), or Monster.com.

Some technical considerations:

- Electronic résumés must be written in American Standard Code for Information Interchange (ASCII), which is simply a plain-text format. These characters are universally recognized so that every computer can accurately read and understand them. To create an ASCII file of your current résumé, open your document, then save it as a text or ASCII file. This will eliminate all formatting. Edit as needed using your computer's text editor application.
- Use a standard-width typeface. Courier is a good choice because it is the font associated with ASCII in most systems.
- Use a font size of 11 to 14 points. A 12-point font is considered standard.
- Your margin should be left-justified.
- Do not exceed sixty-five characters per line because the word-wrap function doesn't operate in ASCII.
- Do not use boldface, italics, underlining, bullets, or various font sizes. Instead, use asterisks, plus signs, or all capital letters when you want to emphasize something.
- Avoid graphics and shading.
- Use as many "keywords" as you possibly can. These are words or phrases usually relating to skills or experience that either are specifically used in the job announcement or are popular buzzwords in the industry.
- Minimize abbreviations.
- Your name should be the first line of text.
- Conduct a "test run" by E-mailing your résumé to yourself and a friend before you send it to the employer. See how it transmits, and make any changes you need to. Continue to test it until it's exactly how you want it to look.
- Unless an employer specifically requests that you send the résumé in the form of an attachment, don't. Employers can encounter problems opening a document as an attachment, and there are always viruses to consider.
- Don't forget your cover letter. Send it along with your résumé as a single message.

Scannable Résumés

Some companies are relying on technology to narrow the candidate pool for available job openings. Electronic Applicant Tracking uses imaging to scan, sort, and store résumé elements in a database. Then, through OCR (Optical Character Recognition) software, the computer scans the résumés for keywords and phrases. To have the best chance at getting an interview, you want to increase the number of "hits"—matches of your skills, abilities, experience, and education to those the computer is scanning for—your résumé will get. You can see how critical using the right keywords is for this type of résumé.

Technical considerations include:

- Again, do not use boldface (newer systems may read this OK, but many older ones won't), italics, underlining, bullets, shading, graphics, or multiple font sizes. Instead, for emphasis, use asterisks, plus signs, or all capital letters. Minimize abbreviations.
- Use a popular typeface such as Courier, Helvetica, Ariel, or Palatino. Avoid decorative fonts.
- Font size should be between 11 and 14 points.
- Do not compress the spacing between letters.
- Use horizontal and vertical lines sparingly; the computer may misread them as the letters L or I.
- Left-justify the text.
- Do not use parentheses or brackets around telephone numbers, and be sure your phone number is on its own line of text.
- Your name should be the first line of text and on its own line. If your résumé is longer than one page, be sure to put your name on the top of all pages.
- Use a traditional résumé structure. The chronological format may work best.
- Use nouns that are skill-focused, such as management, writer, and programming. This is different from traditional paper résumés, which use action-oriented verbs.
- Laser printers produce the finest copies. Avoid dot-matrix printers.
- Use standard, light-colored paper with text on one side only. Since the higher the contrast, the better, your best choice is black ink on white paper.
- Always send original copies. If you must fax, set the fax on fine mode, not standard.

- Do not staple or fold your résumé. This can confuse the computer.
- Before you send your scannable résumé, be certain the employer uses this technology. If you can't determine this, you may want to send two versions (scannable and traditional) to be sure your résumé gets considered.

Résumé Production and Other Tips

An ink-jet printer is the preferred option for printing your résumé. Begin by printing just a few copies. You may find a small error or you may simply want to make some changes, and it is less frustrating and less expensive if you print in small batches.

Résumé paper color should be carefully chosen. You should consider the types of employers who will receive your résumé and the types of positions for which you are applying. Use white or ivory paper for traditional or conservative employers or for higher-level positions.

Black ink on sharp, white paper can be harsh on the reader's eyes. Think about an ivory or cream paper that will provide less contrast and be easier to read. Pink, green, and blue tints should generally be avoided.

Many résumé writers buy packages of matching envelopes and cover sheet stationery that, although not absolutely necessary, help convey a professional impression.

If you'll be producing many cover letters at home, be sure you have high-quality printing equipment. Learn standard envelope formats for business, and retain a copy of every cover letter you send out. You can use the copies to take notes of any telephone conversations that may occur.

If attending a job fair, either carry a briefcase or place your résumé in a nicely covered legal-size pad holder.

The Cover Letter

The cover letter provides you with the opportunity to tailor your résumé by telling the prospective employer how you can be a benefit to the organization. It allows you to highlight aspects of your background that are not already discussed in your résumé and that might be especially relevant to the organization you are contacting or to the position you are seeking. Every résumé should have a cover letter enclosed when you send it out. Unlike the résumé, which may be mass-produced, a cover letter is most effective when

Exhibit 2.6
COVER LETTER FORMAT

Your Street Address
Your Town, State, Zip
Phone Number
Fax Number
E-mail

Date

Name
Title
Organization
Address

Dear _____:

First Paragraph. In this paragraph state the reason for the letter, name the specific position or type of work you are applying for, and indicate from which resource (career services office, website, newspaper, contact, employment service) you learned of this opening. The first paragraph can also be used to inquire about future openings.

Second Paragraph. Indicate why you are interested in this position, the company, or its products or services, and what you can do for the employer. If you are a recent graduate, explain how your academic background makes you a qualified candidate. Try not to repeat the same information found in the résumé.

Third Paragraph. Refer the reader to the enclosed résumé for more detailed information.

Fourth Paragraph. In this paragraph say what you will do to follow up on your letter. For example, state that you will call by a certain date to set up an interview or to find out if the company will be recruiting in your area. Finish by indicating your willingness to answer any questions they may have. Be sure you have provided your phone number.

Sincerely,

Type your name
Enclosure

it is individually prepared and focused on the particular requirements of the organization in question.

A good cover letter should supplement the résumé and motivate the reader to review the résumé. The format shown in Exhibit 2.6 is only a suggestion to help you decide what information to include in writing a cover letter.

Begin the cover letter with your street address six lines down from the top. Leave three to five lines between the date and the name of the person to whom you are addressing the cover letter. Make sure you leave one blank line between the salutation and the body of the letter and between paragraphs. After typing "Sincerely," leave four blank lines and type your name. This should leave plenty of room for your signature. A sample cover letter is shown in Exhibit 2.7.

The following guidelines will help you write good cover letters:

1. Be sure to type your letter neatly; ensure there are no misspellings.
2. Avoid unusual typefaces, such as script.
3. Address the letter to an individual, using the person's name and title. To obtain this information, call the company. If answering a blind newspaper advertisement, address the letter "To Whom It May Concern" or omit the salutation.
4. Be sure your cover letter directly indicates the position you are applying for and tells why you are qualified to fill it.
5. Send the original letter, not a photocopy, with your résumé. Keep a copy for your records.
6. Make your cover letter no more than one page.
7. Include a phone number where you can be reached.
8. Avoid trite language and have someone read the letter over to react to its tone, content, and mechanics.
9. For your own information, record the date you send out each letter and résumé.

Exhibit 2.7
SAMPLE COVER LETTER

435 Winchester Street
Brookline, MA 02146
(617) 555-4434

April 25, 2002

John Sullivan
Director of Personnel
Colonial Williamsburg Foundation
P.O. Drawer T
Williamsburg, VA 23185

Dear Mr. Sullivan:

In May of 2002 I will graduate from Tufts University with a bachelor of science degree in computer programming. I read of your opening for a researcher conversant with Internet search engines in *The Herald* on Sunday, April 24, 2002, and I am very interested in the possibilities it offers. I am writing to explore the opportunity for employment with the Foundation.

The ad indicated you were looking for creative individuals with an interest in U.S. history and good research and communication skills. I believe I possess those qualities. During the summers while in college I worked at Plimoth Plantation in several capacities, including character interpreter and as an assistant in the research department. Through my work there, I learned the importance of possessing good organizational skills and maintaining a positive attitude with coworkers and visitors.

In addition to the various computer courses in my academic program, I felt it important to enroll in some history, anthropology, and psychology courses, focusing particularly on research design and methods. These courses helped me become comfortable with understanding eighteenth-century American culture, and hone my research skills. These accomplishments I believe will help me to represent the Colonial Williamsburg Foundation in a professional and enthusiastic manner.

continued

I would like to meet with you to discuss how my education and experience would be consistent with your needs. I will contact your office next week to discuss the possibility of an interview. In the meantime, if you have any questions or require additional information, please contact me at my home, (617) 555-4434, or via E-mail at JudLevin@xxx.net.

Sincerely,

Judith Levinson
Enclosure

3

Researching Careers

A common question posed to career counselors is "What can I do with my degree?" Even if computer majors know the type of computer work they want to do—programming, systems analysis, database administration, software or hardware design, or even sales and service—they might be unsure of the various job settings in which work is available. Today, almost every type of service, industry, or institution depends on the services of some sort of computer professional. But would you fit in more comfortably at a large corporation or a small private business, or working with the government, in a hospital, an educational institution, or any number of settings? The choices really are limitless.

What Do They Call the Job You Want?

There is every reason to be unaware. One reason for confusion is perhaps a mistaken assumption that a college education provides job training. In most cases it does not. Of course, applied fields such as engineering, management, or education provide specific skills for the workplace as well as an education, whereas most liberal arts degrees simply provide an education. Regardless, your overall college education exposes you to numerous fields of study and teaches you quantitative reasoning, critical thinking, writing, and speaking, all of which can be successfully applied to a number of different job fields. But it still remains up to you to choose a job field and to learn how to articulate the benefits of your education in a way the employer will appreciate.

As indicated in Chapter 1 on self-assessment, your first task is to understand and value what parts of that education you enjoyed and were good at and would continue to enjoy in your life's work. Did your writing courses encourage you in your ability to express yourself in writing? Did you enjoy the research process, and did you find that your work was well received? Did you enjoy any of your required quantitative subjects such as algebra or calculus?

The answers to questions such as these provide clues to skills and interests you bring to the employment market over and above the credential of your degree. In fact, it is not an overstatement to suggest that most employers who demand a college degree immediately look beyond that degree to you as a person and your own individual expression of what you like to do and think you can do for them, regardless of your major.

Collecting Job Titles

The world of employment is a big place, and even seasoned veterans of the job hunt can be surprised about what jobs are to be found in what organizations. You need to become a bit of an explorer and adventurer and be willing to try a variety of techniques to begin a list of possible occupations that might use your talents and education. Once you have a list of possibilities that you are interested in and qualified for, you can move on to find out what kinds of organizations have these job titles.

All employers seeking to hire someone with a computer degree may not be equally desirable to you. You'll find that some employment environments are more attractive to you than others. A computer programmer wanting to work with business systems could do that for a large corporation, a small firm within a corporation, a private concern, or the government, a financial institution, or even in a hospital setting. Each of these environments presents a different "culture" with associated norms in the pace of work, subject matter of interest, and backgrounds of its employees. While the job titles may be the same, not all locations may present the same "fit" for you.

If you majored in computer science, you probably enjoyed the exacting, detailed work you did as part of your degree and naturally think first about systems analysis or computer engineering. But computer science majors with these same skills and interests might go on to teach others their skills or work as software engineers or CAD specialists. Each of these job titles can also be found in a number of different settings.

Take training, for example. Trainers write policy and procedural manuals and actively teach to assist all levels of employees in mastering various tasks and work-related systems. Trainers exist in all large corporations, banks, consumer goods manufacturers, medical diagnostic equipment firms, sales organizations, and any organization that has processes or materials that need to be presented to and learned by the staff.

In reading job descriptions or want ads for any of these positions, you would find your four-year degree a "must." However, the academic major might be less important than your own individual skills in critical thinking, analysis, report writing, public presentations, and interpersonal communication. Even more important than thinking or knowing you have certain skills are your ability to express those skills concretely and the examples you use to illustrate them to an employer.

The best beginning to a job search is to create a list of job titles you might want to pursue, learn more about the nature of the jobs behind those titles, and then discover what kinds of employers hire for those positions. In the following section we'll teach you how to build a job title directory to use in your job search.

Developing a Job Title Directory That Works for You

A job title directory is simply a complete list of all the job titles you are interested in, are intrigued by, or think you are qualified for. After combining the understanding gained through self-assessment with your own individual interests and the skills and talents you've acquired with your degree, you'll soon start to read and recognize a number of occupational titles that seem right for you. There are several resources you can use to develop your list, including computer searches, books, and want ads.

Computerized Interest Inventories. One way to begin your search is to identify a number of jobs that call for your degree and the particular skills and interests you identified as part of the self-assessment process. There are excellent interactive career-guidance programs on the market to help you produce such selected lists of possible job titles. Most of these are available at high schools and colleges and at some larger town and city libraries. Two of the industry leaders are CHOICES and DISCOVER. Both allow you to enter interests, values, educational background, and other information to produce lists of possible occupations and industries. Each of the resources listed here will produce different job title lists. Some job titles will appear again and again, while others will be unique to a particular source. Investigate all of them!

Reference Sources. Books on the market that may be available through your local library or career counseling office also suggest various occupations related to specific majors. The following are only a few of the many good books on the market: *The College Board Guide to 150 Popular College Majors, College Majors and Careers: A Resource Guide for Effective Life Planning* both by Paul Phifer, and *Kaplan's What to Study: 101 Fields in a Flash*. All of these books list possible job titles within the academic major.

For computer majors, the *OOH* lists more than two dozen related job titles. Some are familiar, such as computer programmer or computer engineer, and others are interestingly different, such as database administrator or computer support analyst.

The Bureau of Labor Statistics' employment projections website (bls.gov) is another good resource that allows job seekers to compare occupations on factors such as job openings, earnings, and training requirements.

If, for example, you discover systems analyst as a job title in the *OOH*, you can then go to this site and find information about scores of jobs related to that title. This source adds some depth by presenting statistics in a number of different occupations within that field.

Each job title deserves your consideration. Like removing the layers of an onion, the search for job titles can go on and on! As you spend time doing this activity, you are actually learning more about the value of your degree. What's important in your search at this point is not to become critical or selective but rather to develop as long a list of possibilities as you can. Every source used will help you add new and potentially exciting jobs to your growing list.

Classified Ads. It has been well publicized that the classified ad section of the newspaper represents only about 10 to 15 percent of the current job market. Nevertheless, the weekly classified ads can be a great help to you in your search. Although they may not be the best place to look for a job, they can teach you a lot about the job market. Classified ads provide a good education in job descriptions, duties, responsibilities, and qualifications. In addition, they provide insight into which industries are actively recruiting and some indication of the area's employment market. This is particularly helpful when seeking a position in a specific geographic area and/or a specific field. For your purposes, classified ads are a good source for job titles to add to your list.

Read the Sunday classified ads in a major market newspaper for several weeks in a row. Cut and paste all the ads that interest you and seem to call for something close to your education, skills, experience, and interests. Remember that classified ads are written for what an organization *hopes* to find, you don't have to meet absolutely every criterion. However, if certain requirements are stated as absolute minimums and you cannot meet them, it's best not to waste your time and that of the employer.

The weekly classified want ads exercise is important because these jobs are out in the marketplace. They truly exist, and people with your qualifications are being sought to apply. What's more, many of these advertisements describe the duties and responsibilities of the job advertised and give you a beginning sense of the challenges and opportunities such a position presents. Some will indicate salary, and that will be helpful as well. This information will better define the jobs for you and provide some good material for possible interviews in that field.

Exploring Job Descriptions

Once you've arrived at a solid list of possible job titles that interest you and for which you believe you are somewhat qualified, it's a good idea to do some research on each of these jobs. The preeminent source for such job information is the *Dictionary of Occupational Titles*, or *DOT* (wave.net/upg/immigration/dot_index.html). This directory lists every conceivable job and provides excellent up-to-date information on duties and responsibilities, interactions with associates, and day-to-day assignments and tasks. These descriptions provide a thorough job analysis, but they do not consider the possible employers or the environments in which a job may be performed. So, although a position as public relations officer may be well defined in terms of duties and responsibilities, it does not explain the differences in doing public relations work in a college or a hospital or a factory or a bank. You will need to look somewhere else for work settings.

Learning More About Possible Work Settings

After reading some job descriptions, you may choose to edit and revise your list of job titles once again, discarding those you feel are not suitable and keeping those that continue to hold your interest. Or you may wish to keep your list intact and see where these jobs may be located. For example, if you are interested in public relations and you appear to have those skills and the requisite education, you'll want to know what organizations do public relations. How can you find that out? How much income does someone in public relations make a year and what is the employment potential for the field of public relations?

To answer these and many other questions about your list of job titles, we recommend you try any of the following resources: *Careers Encyclopedia*, the professional societies and resources found throughout this book, *College to Career: The Guide to Job Opportunities*, and the *Occupational Outlook Handbook* (http://stats.bls.gov/ocohome.htm). Each of these resources, in a different way, will help to put the job titles you have selected into an employer context. Perhaps the most extensive discussion is found in the *Occupational Outlook Handbook*, which gives a thorough presentation of the nature of the work, the working conditions, employment statistics, training, other qualifications, and advancement possibilities as well as job outlook and earnings. Related occupations are also detailed, and a select bibliography is provided to help you find additional information.

Continuing with our public relations example, your search through these reference materials would teach you that the public relations jobs you find attractive are available in larger hospitals, financial institutions, most corporations (both consumer goods and industrial goods), media organizations, and colleges and universities.

Networking to Get the Complete Story

You now have not only a list of job titles but also, for each of these job titles, a description of the work involved and a general list of possible employment settings in which to work. You'll want to do some reading and keep talking to friends, colleagues, teachers, and others about the possibilities. Don't neglect to ask if the career office at your college maintains some kind of alumni network. Often such alumni networks will connect you with another graduate from the college who is working in the job title or industry you are seeking information about. These career networkers offer what assistance they can. For some it is a full day "shadowing" the alumnus as he or she goes about the job. Others offer partial-day visits, tours, informational interviews, résumé reviews, job postings, or, if distance prevents a visit, telephone interviews. As fellow graduates, they'll be frank and informative about their own jobs and prospects in their field.

Take them up on their offer and continue to learn all you can about your own personal list of job titles, descriptions, and employment settings. You'll probably continue to edit and refine this list as you learn more about the realities of the job, the possible salary, advancement opportunities, and supply and demand statistics.

In the next section we'll describe how to find the specific organizations that represent these industries and employers so that you can begin to make contact.

Where Are These Jobs, Anyway?

Having a list of job titles that you've designed around your own career interests and skills is an excellent beginning. It means you've really thought about who you are and what you are presenting to the employment market. It has caused you to think seriously about the most appealing environments to work in, and you have identified some employer types that represent these environments.

The research and the thinking that you've done thus far will be used again and again. They will be helpful in writing your résumé and cover letters, in talking about yourself on the telephone to prospective employers, and in answering interview questions.

Now is a good time to begin to narrow the field of job titles and employment sites down to some specific employers to initiate the employment contact.

Finding Out Which Employers Hire People Like You

This section will provide tips, techniques, and specific resources for developing an actual list of specific employers that can be used to make contacts. It is only an outline that you must be prepared to tailor to your own particular needs and according to what you bring to the job search. Once again, it is important to communicate with others along the way exactly what you're looking for and what your goals are for the research you're doing. Librarians, employers, career counselors, friends, friends of friends, business contacts, and bookstore staff will all have helpful information on geographically specific and new resources to aid you in locating employers who'll hire you.

Identifying Information Resources

Your interview wardrobe and your new résumé might have put a dent in your wallet, but the resources you'll need to pursue your job search are available for free (although you may choose to copy materials on a machine instead of taking notes by hand). The categories of information detailed here are not hard to find and are yours for the browsing.

Numerous resources described in this section will help you identify actual employers. Use all of them or any others that you identify as available in your geographic area. As you become experienced in this process, you'll quickly figure out which information sources are helpful and which are not. If you live in a rural area, a well-planned day trip to a major city that includes a college career office, a large college or city library, state and federal employment centers, a chamber of commerce office, and a well-stocked bookstore can produce valuable results.

There are many excellent resources available to help you identify actual job sites. They are categorized into employer directories (usually indexed by product lines and geographic location), geographically based directories (designed to highlight particular cities, regions, or states), career-specific directories (e.g., *Sports MarketPlace*, which lists tens of thousands of firms involved with sports), periodicals and newspapers, targeted job posting publications, and videos. This is by no means meant to be a complete treatment of resources but rather a starting point for identifying useful resources.

Working from the more general references to highly specific resources, we provide a basic list to help you begin your search. Many of these you'll find easily available. In some cases reference librarians and others will suggest even better materials for your particular situation. Start to create your own customized bibliography of job search references. Use copying services to save time and to allow you to carry away information about organizations' missions, locations, company officers, phone numbers, and addresses.

Geographically Based Directories. The Job Bank series published by Bob Adams, Inc. (aip.com) contains detailed entries on each area's major employers, including business activity, address, phone number, and hiring contact name. Many listings specify educational backgrounds being sought in potential employees. Each volume contains a solid discussion of each city's or state's major employment sectors. Organizations are also indexed by industry. Job Bank volumes are available for the following places: Atlanta, Boston, Chicago, Dallas–Ft. Worth, Denver, Detroit, Florida, Houston, Los Angeles, Minneapolis, New York, Ohio, Philadelphia, San Francisco, Seattle, St. Louis, Washington, D.C., and other cities throughout the Northwest.

National Job Bank (careercity.com) lists employers in every state, along with contact names and commonly hired job categories. Included are many small companies often overlooked by other directories. Companies are also indexed by industry. This publication provides information on educational backgrounds sought and lists company benefits.

Periodicals and Newspapers. Several sources are available to help you locate which journals or magazines carry job advertisements in your field. Other resources help you identify opportunities in other parts of the country.

- *Where the Jobs Are: A Comprehensive Directory of 1200 Journals Listing Career Opportunities*
  Links specific occupational titles to corresponding periodicals that carry job listings for your field.
- *Corptech Fast 5000 Company Locator*
  Profiles high technology companies throughout the country. The locator is indexed by company name and city.
- *National Business Employment Weekly* (nbew.com)
  Compiles want ads from four regional editors of the *Wall Street Journal* (http://interactive.wsj.com). Most are business and management positions.
- *National Ad Search* (nationaladsearch.com)
  Reprints ads from seventy-five metropolitan newspapers across the country. Although the focus is on management positions, technical and professional postings are also included. *Caution:* Watch deadline dates carefully on listings, because they may have already passed by the time the ad is printed.
- *The Federal Jobs Digest* (jobsfed.com) and *Federal Career Opportunities* List government positions.
- *World Chamber of Commerce Directory* (chamberofcommerce.org)
  Lists addresses for chambers worldwide, state boards of tourism, convention and visitors' bureaus, and economic development organizations. This information not only helps locate employers but

provides information on employers planning to relocate into a specific geographic area and trade shows that will take place near you where you can meet potential employers.

This list is certainly not exhaustive; use it to begin your job search work.

Targeted Job Posting Publications. Although the resources that follow are national in scope, they are either targeted to one medium of contact (telephone), focused on specific types of jobs, or less comprehensive than the sources previously listed.

- *Job Hotlines USA* (careers.org/topic/01_002.html)
  Pinpoints more than 1,000 hard-to-find telephone numbers for companies and government agencies that use prerecorded job messages and listings. Very few of the telephone numbers listed are toll-free, and sometimes recordings are long, so—callers, beware!
- *The Job Hunter* (jobhunter.com)
  A national biweekly newspaper listing business, arts, media, government, human services, health, community-related, and student services job openings.
- *Current Jobs for Graduates* (graduatejobs.com)
  A national employment listing for liberal arts professions, including editorial positions, management opportunities, museum work, teaching, and nonprofit work.
- *Environmental Opportunities* (ecojobs.com)
  Serves environmental job interests nationwide by listing administrative, marketing, and human resources positions along with education-related jobs and positions directly related to a degree in an environmental field.
- *Y National Vacancy List* (ymcahrm.ns.ca/employed/jobleads.html)
  Shows YMCA professional vacancies, including development, administration, programming, membership, and recreation postings.
- *ARTSearch*
  A national employment service bulletin for the arts, including administration, managerial, marketing, and financial management jobs.
- *Community Jobs*
  An employment newspaper for the nonprofit sector that provides a variety of listings, including project manager, canvas director,

government relations specialist, community organizer, and program instructor.

- *College Placement Council Annual: A Guide to Employment Opportunities for College Graduates*
  An annual guide containing solid job-hunting information and, more important, displaying ads from large corporations actively seeking recent college graduates in all majors. Company profiles provide brief descriptions and available employment opportunities. Contact names and addresses are given. Profiles are indexed by organization name, geographic location, and occupation.
- *National Association of Colleges and Employers* (naceweb.org)
  Job Choices series includes four books: *Planning Job Choices, Job Choices: Diversity Edition, Job Choices in Business,* and *Job Choices in Science, Engineering, and Technology.* The website provides a listing of other books that can be helpful to a wide variety of job seekers.

Videos. You may be one of the many job seekers who likes to get information via a medium other than paper. Many career libraries, public libraries, and career centers in libraries carry an assortment of videos that will help you learn new techniques and get information helpful in the job search.

Locating Information Resources

Throughout these introductory chapters, we have continually referred you to various websites for information on everything from job listings to career information. Using the Web gives you a mobility at your computer that you don't enjoy if you rely solely on books or newspapers or printed journals. Moreover, material on the Web, if the site is maintained, can be up-to-date, which may be crucial if you are looking at a cutting-edge career in which technology changes almost daily. Federal government sites offer the option in some cases of downloading application materials, and many will accept your résumé online.

You'll eventually identify the information resources that work best for you, but make certain you've covered the full range of resources before you begin to rely on a smaller list. Here's a short list of informational sites that many job seekers find helpful:

- Public and college libraries
- College career centers
- Bookstores

- Internet
- Local and state government personnel offices

Each one of these sites offers a collection of resources that will help you get the information you need.

As you meet and talk with service professionals at all these sites, be sure to let them know what you're doing. Inform them of your job search, what you've already accomplished, and what you're looking for. The more people who know you're job seeking, the greater the possibility that someone will have information or know someone who can help you along your way.

Public and College Libraries. Large city libraries, college and university libraries, and even well-supported town library collections contain a variety of resources to help you conduct a job search. It is not uncommon for libraries to have separate "vocational choices" sections with books, tapes, computer terminals, and associated materials relating to job search and selection. Some are now even making résumé-creation software available for use by patrons.

Some of the publications we name throughout this book are expensive reference items that are rarely purchased by individuals. In addition, libraries carry a wide range of newspapers and telephone yellow pages as well as the usual array of books. If resources are not immediately available, many libraries have loan arrangements with other facilities and can make information available to you relatively quickly.

Take advantage not only of the reference collections but also of the skilled and informed staff. Let them know exactly what you are looking for, and they'll have their own suggestions. You'll be visiting the library frequently, and the reference staff will soon come to know who you are and what you're working on. They'll be part of your job search network!

College Career Centers. Career libraries, which are found in career centers at colleges and universities and sometimes within large public libraries, contain a unique blend of the job search resources housed in other settings. In addition, career libraries often purchase a number of job listing publications, each of which targets a specific industry or type of job. You may find job listings specifically for entry-level positions for your major. Ask about job posting newsletters or newspapers focused on careers in the area that most interests you. Each center will be unique, but you are certain to discover some good sources of jobs.

Most college career libraries now hold growing collections of video material on specific industries and on aspects of your job search process, including dress and appearance, how to manage the luncheon or dinner interview, how to be effective at a job fair, and many other titles. Some larger corporations produce handsome video materials detailing the variety of career paths and opportunities available in their organizations.

Some career libraries also house computer-based career planning and information systems. These interactive computer programs help you to clarify your values and interests and will combine them with your education to provide possible job titles and industry locations. Some even contain extensive lists of graduate school programs.

One specific kind of service a career library will be able to direct you to is computerized job search services. These services, of which there are many, are run by private companies, individual colleges, or consortiums of colleges. They attempt to match qualified job candidates with potential employers. The candidate submits a résumé (or an application) to the service. This information (which can be categorized into hundreds of separate fields of data) is entered into a computer database. Your information is then compared with the information from employers about what they desire in a prospective employee. If there is a match between what they want and what you have indicated you can offer, the job search service or the employer will contact you directly to continue the process.

Computerized job search services can complement an otherwise complete job search program. They are *not*, however, a substitute for the kinds of activities described in this book. They are essentially passive operations that are random in nature. If you have not listed skills, abilities, traits, experiences, or education *exactly* as an employer has listed its needs, there is simply no match.

Consult with the staff members at the career libraries you use. These professionals have been specifically trained to meet the unique needs you present. Often you can just drop in and receive help with general questions, or you may want to set up an appointment to speak one-on-one with a career counselor to gain special assistance.

Every career library is different in size and content, but each can provide valuable information for the job search. Some may even provide limited counseling. If you have not visited the career library at your college or alma mater, call and ask if these collections are still available for your use. Be sure to ask about other services that you can use as well.

If you are not near your own college as you work on your job search, call the career office and inquire about reciprocal agreements with other colleges that are closer to where you live. Very often, your own alma mater can arrange for you to use a limited menu of services at another school. This typically would include access to a career library and job posting information and might include limited counseling.

Bookstores. Any well-stocked bookstore will carry some job search books that are worth buying. Some major stores will even have an extensive section devoted to materials, including excellent videos, related to the job search process. You will also find copies of local newspapers and business magazines. The one advantage that is provided by resources purchased at a bookstore is that you can read and work with the information in the comfort of your own home and do not have to conform to the hours of operation of a library, which can present real difficulties if you are working full-time as you seek employment. A few minutes spent browsing in a bookstore might be a beneficial break from your job search activities and turn up valuable resources.

Internet. The World Wide Web has made the search and retrieval of information faster, and in many cases, more efficient. Using search engines such as Netscape, Yahoo!, Google, AltaVista, or MSN, it is possible to find great quantities of information about careers in general, specific employers, and job openings. The Internet should be an important part of any job search strategy.

Use of keywords and/or topics in your specific discipline to search the Web will open numerous opportunities for insight and further exploration. It is important to not only look at "career" websites such as Monster.com, BrassRing.com, or CareerBuilder.com, but to also read the websites of particular employers. Go beyond reading only their career or employment page. Make sure that you read their pages for customers or clients. Learn how they are promoting themselves to the people who buy or use their services. Pay particular attention to the "news" pages on an employer website. There is a great deal to be learned about an organization by reading its "news" page!

Learning which Internet sites are most accurate and fruitful for your job search will take time, persistence, and caution. There's no doubt about it, the Web is a job hunter's best friend. But it can also be an overwhelmingly abundant source of information—so much information that it becomes difficult to identify what's important and what is not. A simple search under a keyword or phrase can bring up sites that will be very meaningful for you and sites whose information is trivial and irrelevant to your job search. You need a strategy to master the Web, just as we advise a strategy to master the job search. Here are some suggestions:

1. Thoroughly utilize the websites identified throughout this guide. They've been chosen with you in mind, and many of them will be very helpful to you.
2. Begin to build your own portfolio of websites on your computer. Use the "bookmarking" function on your Web browser to build a series of bookmark folders for individual categories of good websites. You may have a folder for "entry-level job ad" sites and another folder for "professional associations," and so on. Start your folders with the sites in this book that seem most helpful to you.
3. Visit your college career center (or ask for reciprocity consideration at a local college) and your nearby local and/or state and university libraries. All of these places have staff who are skilled researchers and can help you locate and identify more sites that are more closely targeted to your growing sense of job direction.
4. Use the E-mail function or Webmaster address that you'll find on many sites. Some sites encourage questions via E-mail. We have found that the response time to E-mail questions for website mailboxes can vary considerably, but more often than not, replies are quite prompt. Sometimes a website will list the E-mail of the "Webmaster" or "Webguru," and we have contacted those individuals with good success as well. So, if you have a question about a website, use these options to get satisfaction.

Local and State Government Personnel Offices. You'll learn that it's most efficient to establish a routine for checking job postings. Searching for a job is a full-time job (or should be!), and you don't want to waste time or feel that you're going around in circles. So, establish a routine by which each week, on the most appropriate day, you check out that day's resources. For example, if you live in a midsize city with a daily paper, you'll probably give the want ads a once-over every morning so that you can act immediately on any good job opening.

The same strategy applies to your local and state government personnel offices. Find out when and how they post jobs, and put those offices on your weekly checklist, so that you don't miss any reasonable openings. Your local municipality's personnel office may simply use a bulletin board in the town hall or a clipboard on a counter in the office. Make these stops part of your weekly routine, and you'll find that people begin to recognize you and become aware of your job search, which could prove to be very helpful. Most local governmental units are required to post jobs in public places for a stated period before the hiring process begins. It should be easy to find out where and how they do this. Keep a close eye on those sites.

State personnel offices are larger, less casual operations, but the principles are the same. State jobs are advertised, and the office can tell you what advertising mechanisms they use—which newspapers, what websites, and when jobs are posted. The personnel offices themselves are worth a visit, if you are close enough. In addition to all the current job postings, many state personnel offices have "spec sheets," which are detailed job specifications of all the positions they are apt to advertise. You could pick up a spec sheet for every job related to your major and keep them in a file for later reference when such a job is advertised.

Many state personnel offices also publish a weekly or biweekly "open recruitment" listing of career opportunities that have not yet been filled. These listings are categorized by job title as well as by branch of government, and often by whether a test is needed to qualify for the position or not. An increasing number of state personnel or human resources offices are online and offer many services on the Web. A fine general website that can help you locate your state personnel office is piperinfo.com/state/index.cfm. While each state's site is different, you can count on access to the state human resources office and sometimes even the human resources offices of many of the state's larger cities. For example, the State of Connecticut lists an additional twenty-seven city sites that each have human resources departmental listings. So, you could search the State of Connecticut Human Resource Office and then jump to the City of Stamford and review city jobs on its site.

Career/Job Fairs. Career and/or job fairs are common occurrences on most college campuses. The career services office usually sponsors one or more of these each year. Specific student organizations and academic departments on campus may sponsor them as well. In addition, commercial organizations will sponsor these events in major cities. Watch the employment section of local newspapers and/or the general career Internet sites for announcements of these events near you.

It is important to begin to attend these as early in your college career as possible. By introducing yourself to recruiters and learning what they look for and value in their top candidates, you can better plan your personal career development throughout your college years. However, if you are getting ready to graduate and will now begin attending these events for the purpose of finding an entry-level position, it is advisable that you use them to not only promote yourself but to learn more about the hiring organizations that recruit from your institution.

In addition to coming prepared to tell the recruiter about yourself and why you are interested in the organization, do some preliminary research on the companies that will be participating in the career or job fair and be prepared to ask the recruiter questions about the ideal candidates whom they seek, the type of opportunities that they offer to entry-level professionals, and their hiring process. In other words, use the career or job fair to increase your knowledge of the organizations in which you think you may have an interest, but do not monopolize the recruiter's time. There are others who will want to talk to the representative as well.

Information Sessions. Many recruiters come to campus and sponsor information sessions either in the school or department or in the student center. Look for these events to be advertised in your school paper and on bulletin boards around campus. Often the recruiters will be interested in specific types of majors. However, if you have researched the company in the library and on the Internet, and feel that you have unique qualifications that match its needs, you should attend.

When attending an information session, bring a résumé that is specifically tailored to the organization sponsoring the session. Dress professionally, whenever possible, but do not let a lab or athletic practice keep you from attending a session sponsored by an organization in which you have a strong interest. Arrive on time and do not attempt to talk to the presenters before the program begins. Listen to the presentation and take notes. After the presentation, ask questions from the audience that will be of general interest to the entire group, not specifically to you. For example, an appropriate question might be "What are the promotional opportunities within your organization?" An inappropriate question might be "I know you are here in the Business School tonight, but do you ever hire my major?"

When the question-and-answer period concludes, go up to the presenter(s) and introduce yourself. Explain briefly why you are interested in the organization and how you believe that your skills and experiences fit, and ask a question that is specific to you. Do not monopolize the presenter's time. Follow up with a letter and résumé after this event and thank the presenter for taking time to answer your questions.

4

Networking

Networking is the process of deliberately establishing relationships to get career-related information or to alert potential employers that you are available for work. Networking is critically important to today's job seeker for two reasons: it will help you get the information you need, and it can help you find out about *all* of the available jobs.

Getting the Information You Need

Networkers will review your résumé and give you feedback on its effectiveness. They will talk about the job you are looking for and give you a candid appraisal of how they see your strengths and weaknesses. If they have a good sense of the industry or the employment sector for that job, you'll get their feelings on future trends in the industry as well. Some networkers will be very forthcoming about salaries, job-hunting techniques, and suggestions for your job search strategy. Many have been known to place calls right from the interview desk to friends and associates who might be interested in you. Each networker will make his or her own contribution, and each will be valuable.

Because organizations must evolve to adapt to current global market needs, the information provided by decision makers within various organizations will be critical to your success as a new job market entrant. For example, you might learn about the concept of virtual organizations from a networker. Virtual organizations coordinate economic activity to deliver value to customers by using resources outside the traditional boundaries of the organization. This concept is being discussed and implemented by chief executive officers of many organizations, including Ford Motor, Dell, and IBM. Networking can help you find out about this and other trends currently affecting the industries under your consideration.

Finding Out About All of the Available Jobs

Not every job that is available at this very moment is advertised for potential applicants to see. This is called the *hidden job market*. Only 15 to 20 percent of all jobs are formally advertised, which means that 80 to 85 percent of available jobs do not appear in published channels. Networking will help you become more knowledgeable about all the employment opportunities available during your job search period.

Although someone you might talk to today doesn't know of any openings within his or her organization, tomorrow or next week or next month an opening may occur. If you've taken the time to show an interest in and knowledge of their organization, if you've shown the company representative how you can help achieve organizational goals and that you can fit into the organization, you'll be one of the first candidates considered for the position.

Networking: A Proactive Approach

Networking is a proactive rather than a reactive approach. You, as a job seeker, are expected to initiate a certain level of activity on your own behalf; you cannot afford to simply respond to jobs listed in the newspaper. Being proactive means building a network of contacts that includes informed and interested decision makers who will provide you with up-to-date knowledge of the current job market and increase your chances of finding out about employment opportunities appropriate for your interests, experience, and level of education.

An old axiom of networking says, "You are only two phone calls away from the information you need." In other words, by talking to enough people, you will quickly come across someone who can offer you help. Start with your professors. Each of them probably has a wide circle of contacts. In their work and travel they might have met someone who can help you or direct you to someone who can.

Control and the Networking Process

In deliberately establishing relationships, the process of networking begins with you in control—*you* are contacting specific individuals. As your network expands and you establish a set of professional relationships, your search for information or jobs will begin to move outside of your total control. A part of the networking process involves others assisting you by gathering information for you or recommending you as a possible job candidate. As additional people become a part of your networking system, you will have less knowledge about activities undertaken on your behalf; you will undoubtedly be contacted by individuals whom you did not initially approach. If you want to function effectively in surprise situations, you must be prepared at all times to talk with strangers about the informational or employment needs that motivated you to become involved in the networking process.

Preparing to Network

In deliberately establishing relationships, maximize your efforts by organizing your approach. Five specific areas in which you can organize your efforts include reviewing your self-assessment, reviewing your research on job sites and organizations, deciding who it is you want to talk to, keeping track of all your efforts, and creating your self-promotion tools.

Review Your Self-Assessment

Your self-assessment is as important a tool in preparing to network as it has been in other aspects of your job search. You have carefully evaluated your personal traits, personal values, economic needs, longer-term goals, skill base, preferred skills, and underdeveloped skills. During the networking process you will be called upon to communicate what you know about yourself and relate it to the information or job you seek. Be sure to review the exercises that you completed in the self-assessment section of this book in preparation for networking. We've explained that you need to assess what skills you have acquired from your major that are of general value to an employer and to be ready to express those in ways employers can appreciate as useful in their own organizations.

Review Research on Job Sites and Organizations

In addition, individuals assisting you will expect that you'll have at least some background information on the occupation or industry of interest to you.

Refer to the appropriate sections of this book and other relevant publications to acquire the background information necessary for effective networking. They'll explain how to identify not only the job titles that might be of interest to you but also what kinds of organizations employ people to do that job. You will develop some sense of working conditions and expectations about duties and responsibilities—all of which will be of help in your networking interviews.

Decide Who It Is You Want to Talk To

Networking cannot begin until you decide who it is that you want to talk to and, in general, what type of information you hope to gain from your contacts. Once you know this, it's time to begin developing a list of contacts. Five useful sources for locating contacts are described here.

College Alumni Network. Most colleges and universities have created a formal network of alumni and friends of the institution who are particularly interested in helping currently enrolled students and graduates of their alma mater gain employment-related information.

> The computer science major covers a broad spectrum of human activity. As a result, you'll find computer graduates employed in every sector of the economy: government, business, and nonprofit. The diversity of employment—as evidenced by an alumni list from your college or university—should be encouraging and informative to the computer graduate. Among a diverse group of alumni, there are likely to be scores of people you would enjoy talking with and even perhaps could meet.

It is usually a simple process to make use of an alumni network. Visit your college's website and locate the alumni office and/or your career center. Either or both sites will have information about your school's alumni network. You'll be provided with information on shadowing experiences, geographic information, or those alumni offering job referrals. If you don't find what you're looking for, don't hesitate to phone or E-mail your career center and ask what they can do to help you connect with an alum.

Alumni networkers may provide some combination of the following services: day-long shadowing experiences, telephone interviews, in-person interviews, information on relocating to given geographic areas, internship information, suggestions on graduate school study, and job vacancy notices.

Networking with alumni can be a valuable experience. Perhaps you are interested in working for a major corporation but are concerned about your degree preparation. Spend a day with an alumnus who works for a similar enterprise, and ask lots of questions about his or her educational training and preparation to give you a more concrete view of your degree's possibilities. A firsthand observation of how this person does the job will be an invaluable tool.

Along with your own observations, the alumnus will have his or her own perspective on the relevance of your training and can give you realistic feedback on your job search concerns.

Present and Former Supervisors. If you believe you are on good terms with present or former job supervisors, they may be an excellent resource for providing information or directing you to appropriate resources that would have information related to your current interests and needs. Additionally, these supervisors probably belong to professional organizations that they might be willing to utilize to get information for you.

For example, if you were interested in working as a computer programmer with a major department store chain and you are currently working as an assistant in a local retail shop, talk with your supervisor or the owner. He or she may belong to the Chamber of Commerce, whose executive director would have information on members affiliated with local branches of the chain. You would probably be able to obtain the names and telephone numbers of these people, thus enabling you to begin the networking process.

Employers in Your Area. Although you may be interested in working in a geographic location different from the one where you currently reside, don't overlook the value of the knowledge and contacts those around you are able to provide. Use the local telephone directory and newspaper to identify the types of organizations you are thinking of working for or professionals who have the kinds of jobs you are interested in. Recently, a call made to a local hospital's financial administrator for information on working in health-care financial administration yielded more pertinent information on training seminars, regional professional organizations, and potential employment sites than a national organization was willing to provide.

Employers in Geographic Areas Where You Hope to Work. If you are thinking about relocating, identifying prospective employers or informational contacts in the new location will be critical to your success. Here are some tips for online searching. First, use a "metasearch" engine to get the most out of your search. Metasearch engines combine several engines into one powerful tool. We frequently use dogpile.com and metasearch.com for this purpose. Try using the city and state as your keywords in a search. *New Haven, Connecticut* will bring you to the city's website with links to the chamber of commerce, member businesses, and other valuable resources. By using looksmart.com you can locate newspapers in any area, and they, too, can provide valuable insight before you relocate. Of course, both dogpile and metasearch can lead you to yellow and white page directories in areas you are considering.

Professional Associations and Organizations. Professional associations and organizations can provide valuable information in several areas: career paths that you might not have considered, qualifications relating to those career choices, publications that list current job openings, and workshops or seminars that will enhance your professional knowledge and skills. They can also be excellent sources for background information on given industries: their health, current problems, and future challenges.

There are several excellent resources available to help you locate professional associations and organizations that would have information to meet your needs. Two especially useful publications are the *Encyclopedia of Associations* and *National Trade and Professional Associations of the United States*.

Keep Track of All Your Efforts

It can be difficult, almost impossible, to remember all the details related to each contact you make during the networking process, so you will want to develop a record-keeping system that works for you. Formalize this process by using your computer to keep a record of the people and organizations you want to contact. You can simply record the contact's name, address, and telephone number, and what information you hope to gain. Each entry might look something like this:

Contact Name	Address	Phone #	Purpose
Mr. Lee Perkins Osaka Branch	13 Muromachi Osaka-shi	73-8906	Local market information

You could record this as a simple Word document and you could still use the "Find" function if you were trying to locate some data and could only recall the firm's name or the contact's name. If you're comfortable with database management and you have some database software on your computer, then you can put information at your fingertips even if you have only the zip code! The point here is not technological sophistication but good record keeping.

Once you have created this initial list, it will be helpful to keep more detailed information as you begin to actually make the contacts. Using the Network Contact Record form in Exhibit 4.1 will help you keep good information on all your network contacts. They'll appreciate your recall of details of your meetings and conversations, and the information will help you to focus your networking efforts.

Create Your Self-Promotion Tools

There are two types of promotional tools that are used in the networking process. The first is a résumé and cover letter, and the second is a one-minute "infomercial," which may be given over the telephone or in person.

Techniques for writing an effective résumé and cover letter are discussed in Chapter 2. Once you have reviewed that material and prepared these important documents, you will have created one of your self-promotion tools.

The one-minute infomercial will demand that you begin tying your interests, abilities, and skills to the people or organizations you want to network with. Think about your goal for making the contact to help you understand what you should say about yourself. You should be able to express yourself easily and convincingly. If, for example, you are contacting an alumnus of your institution to obtain the names of possible employment sites in a distant city, be prepared to discuss why you are interested in moving to that location, the types of jobs you are interested in, and the skills and abilities you possess that will make you a qualified candidate.

To create a meaningful one-minute infomercial, write it out, practice it as if it will be a spoken presentation, rewrite it, and practice it again if necessary until expressing yourself comes easily and is convincing.

Here's a simplified example of an infomercial for use over the telephone:

Hello, Ms. Garcia? My name is Gail Sherman. I am a recent graduate of State College, and I wish to enter the health-care field as a systems analyst. I feel confident that I have many of the skills I understand are valued for this position in health care. I have a strong quantitative background, with good inves-

Exhibit 4.1
NETWORK CONTACT RECORD

Name: (Be certain your spelling is correct.)

Title: (Pick up a business card to be certain of the correct title.)

Employing organization: (Note any parent company or subsidiaries.)

Business mailing address: (This is often different from the street address.)

Business E-mail address: _____

Business telephone number: (Include area code and alternative numbers.)

Business fax number: _____

Source for this contact: (Who referred you, and what is their relationship to

the contact?)

Date of call or letter: (Use plenty of space here to record multiple phone calls

or visits, other employees you may have met, names of

secretaries/receptionists, and so forth.)

Content of discussion: (Keep enough notes here to remind you of the substance

of your visits and telephone conversations in case some

time elapses between contacts.)

Follow-up necessary to continue working with this contact: (Your contact may

request that you send him or her some materials or direct

you to contact an associate. Note any such instructions or

assignments in this space.)

Name of additional networker: (Here you would record the names and phone numbers

Address: of additional contacts met at this employer's site. Often

you will be introduced to many people, some of whom

may indicate a willingness to help in your job search.)

E-mail: _____

Phone: _____

Fax: _____

Name of additional networker: _____

Address: _____

E-mail: _____

Phone: _____

Fax: _____

Name of additional networker: _____

Address: _____

E-mail: _____

Phone: _____

Fax: _____

Date thank-you note written: (May help to date your next contact.)

Follow-up action taken: (Phone calls, visits, additional notes.)

Other miscellaneous notes: (Record any other additional interaction you think may be

important to remember in working with this networking

contact. You will want this form in front of you when

telephoning or just before and after a visit.)

tigative and research skills. What's more, I have excellent interpersonal skills, and I work well under pressure. I understand these are valuable traits in this line of work.

Ms. Garcia, I'm calling you because I still need more information about computer positions in the health-care field. I'm hoping you'll have time to sit down with me for about half an hour and discuss your perspective on careers in systems analysis. There are so many possible settings in which to work as a systems analyst, and I am seeking some advice on which of those settings might be the best bet for my particular combination of skills and experience.

Would you be willing to do that for me? I would greatly appreciate it. I am available most mornings, if that's convenient for you.

It very well may happen that your employer contact wishes you to communicate by E-mail. The infomercial quoted above could easily be rewritten for an E-mail message. You should "cut and paste" your résumé right into the E-mail text itself.

Other effective self-promotion tools include portfolios for those in the arts, writing professions, or teaching. Portfolios show examples of work, photographs of projects or classroom activities, or certificates and credentials that are job related. There may not be an opportunity to use the portfolio during an interview, and it is not something that should be left with the organization. It is designed to be explained and displayed by the creator. However, during some networking meetings, there may be an opportunity to illustrate a point or strengthen a qualification by exhibiting the portfolio.

Beginning the Networking Process

Set the Tone for Your Communications

It can be useful to establish "tone words" for any communications you embark upon. Before making your first telephone call or writing your first letter, decide what you want the person to think of you. If you are networking to try to obtain a job, your tone words might include descriptors such as *genuine, informed,* and *self-knowledgeable.* When you're trying to acquire information, your tone words may have a slightly different focus, such as *courteous, organized, focused,* and *well-spoken.* Use the tone words you establish for your contacts to guide you through the networking process.

Honestly Express Your Intentions

When contacting individuals, it is important to be honest about your reasons for making the contact. Establish your purpose in your own mind and be able and ready to articulate it concisely. Determine an initial agenda, whether it be informational questioning or self-promotion, present it to your contact, and be ready to respond immediately. If you don't adequately prepare before initiating your overture, you may find yourself at a disadvantage if you're asked to immediately begin your informational interview or self-promotion during the first phone conversation or visit.

Start Networking Within Your Circle of Confidence

Once you have organized your approach—by utilizing specific researching methods, creating a system for keeping track of the people you will contact, and developing effective self-promotion tools—you are ready to begin networking. The best way to begin networking is by talking with a group of people you trust and feel comfortable with. This group is usually made up of your family, friends, and career counselors. No matter who is in this inner circle, they will have a special interest in seeing you succeed in your job search. In addition, because they will be easy to talk to, you should try taking some risks in terms of practicing your information-seeking approach. Gain confidence in talking about the strengths you bring to an organization and the underdeveloped skills you feel hinder your candidacy. Be sure to review the section on self-assessment for tips on approaching each of these areas. Ask for critical but constructive feedback from the people in your circle of confidence on the letters you write and the one-minute infomercial you have developed. Evaluate whether you want to make the changes they suggest, then practice the changes on others within this circle.

Stretch the Boundaries of Your Networking Circle of Confidence

Once you have refined the promotional tools you will use to accomplish your networking goals, you will want to make additional contacts. Because you will not know most of these people, it will be a less comfortable activity to undertake. The practice that you gained with your inner circle of trusted friends should have prepared you to now move outside of that comfort zone.

It is said that any information a person needs is only two phone calls away, but the information cannot be gained until you (1) make a reasonable guess about who might have the information you need and (2) pick up the telephone to make the call. Using your network list that includes alumni, instructors, supervisors, employers, and associations, you can begin preparing your list of questions that will allow you to get the information you need. Review the question list that follows and then develop a list of your own.

Questions You Might Want to Ask

1. In the position you now hold, what do you do on a typical day?
2. What are the most interesting aspects of your job?

3. What part of your work do you consider dull or repetitive?
4. What were the jobs you had that led to your present position?
5. How long does it usually take to move from one step to the next in this career path?
6. What is the top position to which you can aspire in this career path?
7. What is the next step in *your* career path?
8. Are there positions in this field that are similar to your position?
9. What are the required qualifications and training for entry-level positions in this field?
10. Are there specific courses a student should take to be qualified to work in this field?
11. What are the entry-level jobs in this field?
12. What types of training are provided to persons entering this field?
13. What are the salary ranges your organization typically offers to entry-level candidates for positions in this field?
14. What special advice would you give a person entering this field?
15. Do you see this field as a growing one?
16. How do you see the content of the entry-level jobs in this field changing over the next two years?
17. What can I do to prepare myself for these changes?
18. What is the best way to obtain a position that will start me on a career in this field?
19. Do you have any information on job specifications and descriptions that I may have?
20. What related occupational fields would you suggest I explore?
21. How could I improve my résumé for a career in this field?
22. Who else would you suggest I talk to, both in your organization and in other organizations?

Questions You Might Have to Answer

To communicate effectively, you must anticipate questions that will be asked of you by the networkers you contact. Review the following list and see if you can easily answer each of these questions. If you cannot, it may be time to revisit the self-assessment process.

1. Where did you get my name, or how did you find out about this organization?
2. What are your career goals?
3. What kind of job are you interested in?
4. What do you know about this organization and this industry?

5. How do you know you're prepared to undertake an entry-level position in this industry?
6. What course work have you done that is related to your career interests?
7. What are your short-term career goals?
8. What are your long-term career goals?
9. Do you plan to obtain additional formal education?
10. What contributions have you made to previous employers?
11. Which of your previous jobs have you enjoyed the most and why?
12. What are you particularly good at doing?
13. What shortcomings have you had to face in previous employment?
14. What are your three greatest strengths?
15. Describe how comfortable you feel with your communication style.

General Networking Tips

Make Every Contact Count. Setting the tone for each interaction is critical. Approaches that will help you communicate in an effective way include politeness, being appreciative of time provided to you, and being prepared and thorough. Remember, *everyone* within an organization has a circle of influence, so be prepared to interact effectively with each person you encounter in the networking process, including secretarial and support staff. Many information or job seekers have thwarted their own efforts by being rude to some individuals they encountered as they networked because they made the incorrect assumption that certain persons were unimportant.

Sometimes your contacts may be surprised at their ability to help you. After meeting and talking with you, they might think they have not offered much in the way of help. A day or two later, however, they may make a contact that would be useful to you and refer you to that person.

With Each Contact, Widen Your Circle of Networkers. Always leave an informational interview with the names of at least two more people who can help you get the information or job that you are seeking. Don't be shy about asking for additional contacts; networking is all about increasing the number of people you can interact with to achieve your goals.

Make Your Own Decisions. As you talk with different people and get answers to the questions you pose, you may hear conflicting information or get conflicting suggestions. Your job is to listen to these "experts" and decide what information and which suggestions will help you achieve *your* goals. Only implement those suggestions that you believe will work for you.

Shutting Down Your Network

As you achieve the goals that motivated your networking activity—getting the information you need or the job you want—the time will come to inactivate all or parts of your network. As you do, be sure to tell your primary supporters about your change in status. Call or write to each one of them and give them as many details about your new status as you feel is necessary to maintain a positive relationship.

Because a network takes on a life of its own, activity undertaken on your behalf will continue even after you cease your efforts. As you get calls or are contacted in some fashion, be sure to inform these networkers about your change in status, and thank them for assistance they have provided.

Information on the latest employment trends indicates that workers will change jobs or careers several times in their lifetime. Networking, then, will be a critical aspect in the span of your professional life. If you carefully and thoughtfully conduct your networking activities during your job search, you will have a solid foundation of experience when you need to network the next time around.

5

Interviewing

Certainly, there can be no one part of the job search process more fraught with anxiety and worry than the interview. Yet seasoned job seekers welcome the interview and will often say, "Just get me an interview and I'm on my way!" They understand that the interview is crucial to the hiring process and equally crucial for them, as job candidates, to have the opportunity of a personal dialogue to add to what the employer may already have learned from the résumé, cover letter, and telephone conversations.

Believe it or not, the interview is to be welcomed, and even enjoyed! It is a perfect opportunity for you, the candidate, to sit down with an employer and express yourself and display who you are and what you want. Of course, it takes thought and planning and a little strategy; after all, it *is* a job interview! But it can be a positive, if not pleasant, experience and one you can look back on and feel confident about your performance and effort.

For many new job seekers, a job, any job, seems a wonderful thing. But seasoned interview veterans know that the job interview is an important step for both sides—the employer and the candidate—to see what each has to offer and whether there is going to be a "fit" of personalities, work styles, and attitudes. And it is this concept of balance in the interview, that both sides have important parts to play, that holds the key to success in mastering this aspect of the job search strategy.

Try to think of the interview as a conversation between two interested and equal partners. You both have important, even vital, information to deliver and to learn. Of course, there's no denying the employer has some leverage, especially in the initial interview for recruitment or any interview scheduled by the candidate and not the recruiter. That should not prevent the interviewee from seeking to play an equal part in what should be a fair exchange of information. Too often the untutored candidate allows the interview to become one-sided. The employer asks all the questions and the candidate simply responds. The ideal would be for two mutually interested parties to sit down and discuss possibilities for each. This is a conversation of significance, and it requires preparation, thought about the tone of the interview, and planning of the nature and details of the information to be exchanged.

Preparing for the Interview

The length of most initial interviews is about thirty minutes. Given the brevity, the information that is exchanged ought to be important. The candidate should be delivering material that the employer cannot discover on the résumé, and in turn, the candidate should be learning things about the employer that he or she could not otherwise find out. After all, if you have only thirty minutes, why waste time on information that is already published? The information exchanged is more than just factual, and both sides will learn much from what they see of each other, as well. How the candidate looks, speaks, and acts are important to the employer. The employer's attention to the interview and awareness of the candidate's résumé, the setting, and the quality of information presented are important to the candidate.

Just as the employer has every right to be disappointed when a prospect is late for the interview, looks unkempt, and seems ill-prepared to answer fairly standard questions, the candidate may be disappointed with an interviewer who isn't ready for the meeting, hasn't learned the basic résumé facts, and is constantly interrupted by telephone calls. In either situation there's good reason to feel let down.

There are many elements to a successful interview, and some of them are not easy to describe or prepare for. Sometimes there is just a chemistry between interviewer and interviewee that brings out the best in both, and a good exchange takes place. But there is much the candidate can do to pave the way for success in terms of his or her résumé, personal appearance, goals, and interview strategy—each of which we will discuss. However, none of this preparation is as important as the time and thought the candidate gives to personal self-assessment.

Self-Assessment
Neither a stunning résumé nor an expensive, well-tailored suit can compensate for candidates who do not know what they want, where they are going,

or why they are interviewing with a particular employer. Self-assessment, the process by which we begin to know and acknowledge our own particular blend of education, experiences, needs, and goals, is not something that can be sorted out the weekend before a major interview. Of all the elements of interview preparation, this one requires the longest lead time and cannot be faked.

Because the time allotted for most interviews is brief, it is all the more important for job candidates to understand and express succinctly why they are there and what they have to offer. This is not a time for undue modesty (or for braggadocio either); it is a time for a compelling, reasoned statement of why you feel that you and this employer might make a good match. It means you have to have thought about your skills, interests, and attributes; related those to your life experiences and your own history of challenges and opportunities; and determined what that indicates about your strengths, preferences, values, and areas needing further development.

A common complaint of employers is that many candidates didn't take advantage of the interview time; they didn't seem to know why they were there or what they wanted. When candidates are asked to talk about themselves and their work-related skills and attributes, employers don't want to be faced with shyness or embarrassed laughter; they need to know about you so they can make a fair determination of you and your competition. If you don't take advantage of the opportunity to make a case for your employability, you can be certain the person ahead of you has or the person after you will, and it will be on the strength of those impressions that the employer will hire.

If you need some assistance with self-assessment issues, refer to Chapter 1. Included are suggested exercises that can be done as needed, such as making up an experiential diary and extracting obvious strengths and weaknesses from past experiences. These simple assignments will help you look at past activities as collections of tasks with accompanying skills and responsibilities. Don't overlook your high school or college career office. Many offer personal counseling on self-assessment issues and may provide testing instruments such as the *Myers-Briggs Type Indicator* (*MBTI*), the *Harrington-O'Shea Career Decision-Making System* (*CDM*), the *Strong Interest Inventory* (*SII*), or any other of a wide selection of assessment tools that can help you clarify some of these issues prior to the interview stage of your job search.

The Résumé

Résumé preparation has been discussed in detail, and some basic examples of various types were provided. In this section we want to concentrate on how best to use your résumé in the interview. In most cases the employer will have seen the résumé prior to the interview, and, in fact, it may well have been the quality of that résumé that secured the interview opportunity.

An interview is a conversation, however, and not an exercise in reading. So, if the employer hasn't seen your résumé and you have brought it along to the interview, wait until asked or until the end of the interview to offer it. Otherwise, you may find yourself staring at the back of your résumé and simply answering "yes" and "no" to a series of questions drawn from that document.

Sometimes an interviewer is not prepared and does not know or recall the contents of the résumé and may use the résumé to a greater or lesser degree as a "prompt" during the interview. It is for you to judge what that may indicate about the individual performing the interview or the employer. If your interviewer seems surprised by the scheduled meeting, relies on the résumé to an inordinate degree, and seems otherwise unfamiliar with your background, this lack of preparation for the hiring process could well be a symptom of general management disorganization or may simply be the result of poor planning on the part of one individual. It is your responsibility as a potential employee to be aware of these signals and make your decisions accordingly.

In any event, it is perfectly acceptable for you to get the conversation back to a more interpersonal style by saying something like, "Mr. Lewis, you might be interested in some recent programming experience I gained in an internship that is not detailed on my résumé. May I tell you about it?" This can return the interview to two people talking to each other, not one reading and the other responding.

By all means, bring at least one copy of your résumé to the interview. Occasionally, at the close of an interview, an interviewer will express an interest in circulating a résumé to several departments, and you could then offer the copy you brought. Sometimes, an interview appointment provides an opportunity to meet others in the organization who may express an interest in you and your background, and it may be helpful to follow up with a copy of your résumé. Our best advice, however, is to keep it out of sight until needed or requested.

Appearance

Although many of the absolute rules that once dominated the advice offered to job candidates about appearance have now been moderated significantly, conservative is still the watchword unless you are interviewing in a fashion-related industry. For men, conservative translates into a well-cut dark suit with appropriate tie, hosiery, and dress shirt. A wise strategy for the male job seeker looking for a good but not expensive suit would be to try the men's department of a major department store. They usually carry a good range of sizes, fabrics, and prices; offer professional sales help; provide free tailoring; and have associated departments for putting together a professional look.

For women, there is more latitude. Business suits are still popular, but they have become more feminine in color and styling with a variety of jacket and skirt lengths. In addition to suits, better-quality dresses are now worn in many environments and, with the correct accessories, can be most appropriate. Company literature, professional magazines, the business section of major newspapers, and television interviews can all give clues about what is being worn in different employer environments.

Both men and women need to pay attention to issues such as hair, jewelry, and makeup; these are often what separates the candidate in appearance from the professional workforce. It seems particularly difficult for the young job seeker to give up certain hairstyles, eyeglass fashions, and jewelry habits, yet those can be important to the employer who is concerned with your ability to successfully make the transition into the organization. Candidates often find the best strategy is to dress conservatively until they find employment. Once employed and familiar with the norms within your organization, you can begin to determine a look that you enjoy, works for you, and fits your organization.

Choose clothes that suit your body type, fit well, and flatter you. Feel good about the way you look! The interview day is not the best time for a new hairdo, a new pair of shoes, or any other change that will distract you or cause you to be self-conscious. Arrive a bit early to avoid being rushed, and ask the receptionist to direct you to a restroom for any last-minute adjustments of hair and clothes.

Employer Information

Whether your interview is for graduate school admission, an overseas corporate position, or a position with a local company, it is important to know something about the employer or the organization. Keeping in mind that the interview is relatively brief and that you will hopefully have other interviews with other organizations, it is important to keep your research in proportion. If secondary interviews are called for, you will have additional time to do further research. For the first interview, it is helpful to know the organization's mission, goals, size, scope of operations, and so forth. Your research may uncover recent areas of challenge or particular successes that may help to fuel the interview. Use the "What Do They Call the Job You Want?" section of Chapter 3, your library, and your career or guidance office to help you locate this information in the most efficient way possible. Don't be shy in asking advice of these counseling and guidance professionals on how best to spend your preparation time. With some practice, you'll soon learn how much information is enough and which kinds of information are most useful to you.

Interview Content

We've already discussed how it can help to think of the interview as an important conversation—one that, as with any conversation, you want to find pleasant and interesting and to leave you with a good feeling. But because this conversation is especially important, the information that's exchanged is critical to its success. What do you want them to know about you? What do you need to know about them? What interview technique do you need to particularly pay attention to? How do you want to manage the close of the interview? What steps will follow in the hiring process?

Except for the professional interviewer, most of us find interviewing stressful and anxiety-provoking. Developing a strategy before you begin interviewing will help you relieve some stress and anxiety. One particular strategy that has worked for many and may work for you is interviewing by objective. Before you interview, write down three to five goals you would like to achieve for that interview. They may be technique goals: smile a little more, have a firmer handshake, be sure to ask about the next stage in the interview process before leaving. They may be content-oriented goals: find out about the company's current challenges and opportunities; be sure to speak of your recent research, writing experiences, or foreign travel. Whatever your goals, jot down a few of them as goals for each interview.

Most people find that in trying to achieve these few goals, their interviewing technique becomes more organized and focused. After the interview, the most common question friends and family ask is "How did it go?" With this technique, you have an indication of whether you met *your* goals for the meeting, not just some vague idea of how it went. Chances are, if you accomplished what you wanted to, it improved the quality of the entire interview. As you continue to interview, you will want to revise your goals to continue improving your interview skills.

Now, add to the concept of the significant conversation the idea of a beginning, a middle, and a closing and you will have two thoughts that will give your interview a distinctive character. Be sure to make your introduction warm and cordial. Say your full name (and if it's a difficult-to-pronounce name, help the interviewer to pronounce it) and make certain you know your interviewer's name and how to pronounce it. Most interviews begin with some "soft talk" about the weather, chat about the candidate's trip to the interview site, or national events. This is done as a courtesy to relax both you and the interviewer, to get you talking, and to generally try to defuse the atmosphere of excessive tension. Try to be yourself, engage in the conversation, and don't try to second-guess the interviewer. This is simply what it appears to be—casual conversation.

Once you and the interviewer move on to exchange more serious information in the middle part of the interview, the two most important concerns become your ability to handle challenging questions and your success at asking meaningful ones. Interviewer questions will probably fall into one of three categories: personal assessment and career direction, academic assessment, and knowledge of the employer. The following are some examples of questions in each category:

Personal Assessment and Career Direction
1. How would you describe yourself?
2. What motivates you to put forth your best effort?
3. In what kind of work environment are you most comfortable?
4. What do you consider to be your greatest strengths and weaknesses?
5. How well do you work under pressure?
6. What qualifications do you have that make you think you will be successful in this career?
7. Will you relocate? What do you feel would be the most difficult aspect of relocating?
8. Are you willing to travel?
9. Why should I hire you?

Academic Assessment
1. Why did you select your college or university?
2. What changes would you make at your alma mater?
3. What led you to choose your major?

4. What subjects did you like best and least? Why?
5. If you could, how would you plan your academic study differently? Why?
6. Describe your most rewarding college experience.
7. How has your college experience prepared you for this career?
8. Do you think that your grades are a good indication of your ability to succeed with this organization?
9. Do you have plans for continued study?

Knowledge of the Employer

1. If you were hiring a graduate of your school for this position, what qualities would you look for?
2. What do you think it takes to be successful in an organization like ours?
3. In what ways do you think you can make a contribution to our organization?
4. Why did you choose to seek a position with this organization?

The interviewer wants a response to each question but is also gauging your enthusiasm, preparedness, and willingness to communicate. In each response you should provide some information about yourself that can be related to the employer's needs. A common mistake is to give too much information. Answer each question completely, but be careful not to run on too long with extensive details or examples.

Questions About Underdeveloped Skills

Most employers interview people who have met some minimum criteria of education and experience. They interview candidates to see who they are, to learn what kind of personality they exhibit, and to get some sense of how this person might fit into the existing organization. It may be that you are asked about skills the employer hopes to find and that you have not documented. Maybe it's grant-writing experience, knowledge of the European political system, or a knowledge of the film world.

To questions about skills and experiences you don't have, answer honestly and forthrightly and try to offer some additional information about skills you do have. For example, perhaps the employer is disappointed you have no grant-writing experience. An honest answer may be as follows:

No, unfortunately, I was never in a position to acquire those skills. I do understand something of the complexities of the grant-writing process and feel confident that my attention to detail, careful reading skills, and strong writing would make grants a wonderful challenge in a new job. I think I could get up on the learning curve quickly.

The employer hears an honest admission of lack of experience but is reassured by some specific skill details that do relate to grant writing and a confident manner that suggests enthusiasm and interest in a challenge.

For many students, questions about their possible contribution to an employer's organization can prove challenging. Because your education has probably not included specific training for a job, you need to review your academic record and select capabilities you have developed in your major that an employer can appreciate. For example, perhaps you read well and can analyze and condense what you've read into smaller, more focused pieces. That could be valuable. Or maybe you did some serious research and you know you have valuable investigative skills. Your public speaking might be highly developed and you might use visual aids appropriately and effectively. Or maybe your skill at correspondence, memos, and messages is effective. Whatever it is, you must take it out of the academic context and put it into a new, employer-friendly context so your interviewer can best judge how you could help the organization.

Exhibiting knowledge of the organization will, without a doubt, show the interviewer that you are interested enough in the available position to have done some legwork in preparation for the interview. Remember, it is not necessary to know every detail of the organization's history but rather to have a general knowledge about why it is in business and how the industry is faring.

Sometime during the interview, generally after the midway point, you'll be asked if you have any questions for the interviewer. Your questions will tell the employer much about your attitude and your desire to understand the organization's expectations so you can compare them to your own strengths. The following are some selected questions you might want to ask:

1. What are the main responsibilities of the position?
2. What are the opportunities and challenges associated with this position?
3. Could you outline some possible career paths beginning with this position?
4. How regularly do performance evaluations occur?
5. What is the communication style of the organization? (meetings, memos, and so forth)
6. What would a typical day in this position be like for me?

7. What kinds of opportunities might exist for me to improve my professional skills within the organization?
8. What have been some of the interesting challenges and opportunities your organization has recently faced?

Most interviews draw to a natural closing point, so be careful not to prolong the discussion. At a signal from the interviewer, wind up your presentation, express your appreciation for the opportunity, and be sure to ask what the next stage in the process will be. When can you expect to hear from them? Will they be conducting second-tier interviews? If you are interested and haven't heard, would they mind a phone call? Be sure to collect a business card with the name and phone number of your interviewer. On your way out, you might have an opportunity to pick up organizational literature you haven't seen before.

With the right preparation—a thorough self-assessment, professional clothing, and employer information—you'll be able to set and achieve the goals you have established for the interview process.

6

Networking or Interview Follow-Up

Quite often there is a considerable time lag between interviewing for a position and being hired or, in the case of the networker, between your phone call or letter to a possible contact and the opportunity of a meeting. This can be frustrating. "Why aren't they contacting me?" "I thought I'd get another interview, but no one has telephoned." "Am I out of the running?" You don't know what is happening.

Consider the Differing Perspectives

Of course, there is another perspective—that of the networker or hiring organization. Organizations are complex, with multiple tasks that need to be accomplished each day. Hiring is a discrete activity that does not occur as frequently as other job assignments. The hiring process might have to take second place to other, more immediate organizational needs. Although it may be very important to you, and it is certainly ultimately significant to the employer, other issues such as fiscal management, planning and product development, employer vacation periods, or financial constraints may prevent an organization or individual within that organization from acting on your employment or your request for information as quickly as you or they would prefer.

Use Your Communication Skills

Good communication is essential here to resolve any anxieties, and the responsibility is on you, the job or information seeker. Too many job seekers and networkers offer as an excuse that they don't want to "bother" the organization by writing letters or calling. Let us assure you here and now, once and for all, that if you are troubling an organization by over-communicating, someone will indicate that situation to you quite clearly. If not, you can only assume you are a worthwhile prospect and the employer appreciates being reminded of your availability and interest. Let's look at follow-up practices in the job interview process and the networking situation separately.

Following Up on the Employment Interview

A brief thank-you note following an interview is an excellent and polite way to begin a series of follow-up communications with a potential employer with whom you have interviewed and want to remain in touch. It should be just that—a thank-you for a good meeting. If you failed to mention some fact or experience during your interview that you think might add to your candidacy, you may use this note to do that. However, this should be essentially a note whose overall tone is appreciative and, if appropriate, indicative of a continuing interest in pursuing any opportunity that may exist with that organization. It is one of the few pieces of business correspondence that may be handwritten, but always use plain, good-quality, standard-size paper.

If, however, at this point you are no longer interested in the employer, the thank-you note is an appropriate time to indicate that. You are under no obligation to identify any reason for not continuing to pursue employment with that organization, but if you are so inclined to indicate your professional reasons (pursuing other employers more akin to your interests, looking for greater income production than this employer can provide, a different geographic location), you certainly may. It should not be written with an eye to negotiation, for it will not be interpreted as such.

As part of your interview closing, you should have taken the initiative to establish lines of communication for continuing information about your candidacy. If you asked permission to telephone, wait a week following your thank-you note, then telephone your contact simply to inquire how things are progressing on your employment status. The feedback you receive here should be taken at face value. If your interviewer simply has no information, he or she will tell you so and indicate whether you should call again and when. Don't be discouraged if this should continue over some period of time.

If during this time something occurs that you think improves or changes your candidacy (some new qualification or experience you may have had), including any offers from other organizations, by all means telephone or write to inform the employer about this. In the case of an offer from a competing but less desirable or equally desirable organization, telephone your contact, explain what has happened, express your real interest in the organization, and inquire whether some determination on your employment might be made before you must respond to this other offer. An organization that is truly interested in you may be moved to make a decision about your candidacy. Equally possible is the scenario in which they are not yet ready to make a decision and so advise you to take the offer that has been presented. Again, you have no ethical alternative but to deal with the information presented in a straightforward manner.

When accepting other employment, be sure to contact any employers still actively considering you and inform them of your new job. Thank them graciously for their consideration. There are many other job seekers out there just like you who will benefit from having their candidacy improved when others bow out of the race. Who knows, you might at some future time have occasion to interact professionally with one of the organizations with which you sought employment. How embarrassing it would be to have someone remember you as the candidate who failed to notify them that you were taking a job elsewhere!

In all of your follow-up communications, keep good notes of whom you spoke with, when you called, and any instructions that were given about return communications. This will prevent any misunderstandings and provide you with good records of what has transpired.

Following Up on the Network Contact

Far more common than the forgotten follow-up after an interview is the situation where a good network contact is allowed to lapse. Good communications are the essence of a network, and follow-up is not so much a matter of courtesy here as it is a necessity. In networking for job information and contacts, you are the active network link. Without you, and without continual contact from you, there is no network. You and your need for employment are often the only shared elements among members of the network. Because network contacts were made regardless of the availability of any particular employment, it is incumbent upon the job seeker, if not simple common sense, to stay in regular communication with the network if you want to be considered for any future job opportunities.

This brings up the issue of responsibility, which is likewise very clear. The job seeker initiates network contacts and is responsible for maintaining those contacts; therefore, the entire responsibility for the network belongs with him or her. This becomes patently obvious if the network is left unattended. It very shortly falls out of existence because it cannot survive without careful attention by the networker.

You have many ways to keep the lines of communication open and to attempt to interest the network in you as a possible employee. You are limited only by your own enthusiasm for members of the network and your creativity. However, you as a networker are well advised to keep good records of whom you have met and contacted in each organization. Be sure to send thank-you notes to anyone who has spent any time with you, whether it was an E-mail message containing information or advice, a quick tour of a department, or a sit-down informational interview. All of these thank-you notes should, in addition to their ostensible reason, add some information about you and your particular combination of strengths and attributes.

You can contact your network at any time to convey continued interest, to comment on some recent article you came across concerning an organization, to add information about your training or changes in your qualifications, to ask advice or seek guidance in your job search, or to request referrals to other possible network opportunities. Sometimes just a simple note to network members reminding them of your job search, indicating that you have been using their advice, and noting that you are still actively pursuing leads and hope to continue to interact with them is enough to keep communications alive.

The Internet has opened up the world of networking. You may be able to find networkers who graduated from your high school or from the college you're attending, who live in a geographic region where you hope to work, or who are employed in a given industry. The Internet makes it easy to reach out to many people, but don't let this perceived ease lull you into complacency. Internet networking demands the same level of preparation as the more traditional forms of networking.

Because networks have been abused in the past, it's important that your conduct be above reproach. Networks are exploratory options; they are not backdoor access to employers. The network works best for someone who is exploring a new industry or making a transition into a new area of employment and who needs to find information or to alert people to his or her search activity. Always be candid and direct with contacts in expressing the purpose of your E-mail, call, or letter and your interest in their help or information about their organization. In follow-up contacts keep the tone professional and direct. Your honesty will be appreciated, and people will respond as best they can if your qualifications appear to meet their forth-coming needs. The network does not owe you anything, and that tone should be clear to each person you meet.

Feedback from Follow-Ups

A network contact may prove to be miscalculated. Perhaps you were referred to someone and it became clear that your goals and his or her particular needs did not make a good match. Or the network contact may simply not be in a position to provide you with the information you are seeking. Or in some unfortunate situations, the party may become annoyed by being contacted for this purpose. In such a situation, many job seekers simply say "Thank you" and move on.

If the contact is simply not the right connection, but the individual you are speaking with is not annoyed by the call, it might be a better tactic to express regret that the contact was misplaced and then tell the person what you are seeking and ask for his or her advice or possible suggestions as to a next step. The more people who are aware that you are seeking employment, the better your chances of connecting, and that is the purpose of a network. Most people in a profession have excellent knowledge of their field and vary-ing amounts of expertise in areas tangent to their own. Use their expertise and seek some guidance before you dissolve the contact. You may be pleas-antly surprised.

Occasionally, networkers will express the feeling that they have done as much as they can or provided all the information that is available to them. This may be a cue that they would like to be released from your network. Be alert to such attempts to terminate, graciously thank the individual by letter, and move on in your network development. A network is always changing, adding and losing members, and you want the network to be com-posed only of those who are actively interested in supporting you.

A Final Point on Networking for Computer Science Majors

No matter where a computer major might consider working, your contacts will critically evaluate all of your written and oral communications. Place special emphasis on the quality of your interactions with people who are in a position to help you in your job search.

In your telephone communications, interview presentation, and follow-up correspondence or E-mail, your style and personality, as evidenced in your spoken and written use of English, will be an important part of the portfolio of impressions you create.

7

Job Offer Considerations

For many recent college graduates, the thrill of their first job and, for some, the most substantial regular income they have ever earned seems an excess of good fortune coming at once. To question that first income or to be critical in any way of the conditions of employment at the time of the initial offer seems like looking a gift horse in the mouth. It doesn't seem to occur to many new hires even to attempt to negotiate any aspect of their first job. And, as many employers who deal with entry-level jobs for recent college graduates will readily confirm, the reality is that there simply isn't much movement in salary available to these new college recruits. The entry-level hire generally does not have an employment track record on a professional level to provide any leverage for negotiation. Real negotiations on salary, benefits, retirement provisions, and so forth come to those with significant employment records at higher income levels.

Of course, the job offer is more than just money. It can be composed of geographic assignment, duties and responsibilities, training, benefits, health and medical insurance, educational assistance, car allowance or company vehicle, and a host of other items. All of this is generally detailed in the formal letter that presents the final job offer. In most cases this is a follow-up to a personal phone call from the employer representative who has been principally responsible for your hiring process.

That initial telephone offer is certainly binding as a verbal agreement, but most firms follow up with a detailed letter outlining the most significant parts of your employment contract. You may, of course, choose to respond immediately at the time of the telephone offer (which would be considered a binding oral contract), but you will also be required to formally answer the letter of offer with a letter of acceptance, restating the salient elements of the employer's description of your position, salary, and benefits. This ensures that both parties are clear on the terms and conditions of employment and remuneration and any other outstanding aspects of the job offer.

Is This the Job You Want?

Most new employees will respond affirmatively in writing, glad to be in the position to accept employment. If you've worked hard to get the offer and the job market is tight, other offers may not be in sight, so you will say, "Yes, I accept!" What is important here is that the job offer you accept be one that does fit your particular needs, values, and interests as you've outlined them in your self-assessment process. Moreover, it should be a job that will not only use your skills and education but also challenge you to develop new skills and talents.

Jobs are sometimes accepted too hastily, for the wrong reasons, and without proper scrutiny by the applicant. For example, an individual might readily accept a sales job only to find the continual rejection by potential clients unendurable. An office worker might realize within weeks the constraints of a desk job and yearn for more activity. Employment is an important part of our lives. It is, for most of our adult lives, our most continuous productive activity. We want to make good choices based on the right criteria.

If you have a low tolerance for risk, a job based on commission will certainly be very anxiety-provoking. If being near your family is important, issues of relocation could present a decision crisis for you. If you're an adventurous person, a job with frequent travel would provide needed excitement and be very desirable. The importance of income, the need to continue your education, your personal health situation—all of these have an impact on whether the job you are considering will ultimately meet your needs. Unless you've spent some time understanding and thinking about these issues, it will be difficult to evaluate offers you do receive.

More important, if you make a decision that you cannot tolerate and feel you must leave that job, you will then have both unemployment and self-esteem issues to contend with. These will combine to make the next job search tough going, indeed. So make your acceptance a carefully considered decision.

Negotiating Your Offer

It may be that there is some aspect of your job offer that is not particularly attractive to you. Perhaps there is no relocation allotment to help you move your possessions, and this presents some financial hardship for you. It may be that the health insurance is less than you had hoped. Your initial assignment may be different from what you expected, either in its location or in the duties and responsibilities that comprise it. Or it may simply be that the salary is less than you anticipated. Other considerations may be your official starting date of employment, vacation time, evening hours, dates of training programs or schools, and other concerns.

If you are considering not accepting the job because of some item or items in the job offer "package" that do not meet your needs, you should know that most employers emphatically wish that you would bring that issue to their attention. It may be that the employer can alter it to make the offer more agreeable for you. In some cases it cannot be changed. In any event the employer would generally like to have the opportunity to try to remedy a difficulty rather than risk losing a good potential employee over an issue that might have been resolved. After all, they have spent time and funds in securing your services, and they certainly deserve an opportunity to resolve any possible differences.

Honesty is the best approach in discussing any objections or uneasiness you might have over the employer's offer. Having received your formal offer in writing, contact your employer representative and indicate your particular dissatisfaction in a straightforward manner. For example, you might explain that while you are very interested in being employed by this organization, the salary (or any other benefit) is less than you have determined you require. State the terms you need, and listen to the response. You may be asked to put this in writing, or you may be asked to hold off until the firm can decide on a response. If you are dealing with a senior representative of the organization, one who has been involved in hiring for some time, you may get an immediate response or a solid indication of possible outcomes.

Perhaps the issue is one of relocation. Your initial assignment is in the Midwest, and because you had indicated a strong West Coast preference, you are surprised at the actual assignment. You might simply indicate that while you understand the need for the company to assign you based on its needs, you are disappointed and had hoped to be placed on the West Coast. You could inquire if that were still possible and, if not, would it be reasonable to expect a West Coast relocation in the future.

If your request is presented in a reasonable way, most employers will not see this as jeopardizing your offer. If they can agree to your proposal, they will. If not, they will simply tell you so, and you may choose to continue your candidacy with them or remove yourself from consideration. The choice will be up to you.

Some firms will adjust benefits within their parameters to meet the candidate's need if at all possible. If a candidate requires a relocation cost allowance, he or she may be asked to forgo tuition benefits for the first year to accomplish this adjustment. An increase in life insurance may be adjusted by some other benefit trade-off; perhaps a family dental plan is not needed. In these decisions you are called upon, sometimes under time pressure, to know how you value these issues and how important each is to you.

Many employers find they are more comfortable negotiating for candidates who have unique qualifications or who bring especially needed expertise to the organization. Employers hiring large numbers of entry-level college graduates may be far more reluctant to accommodate any changes in offer conditions. They are well supplied with candidates with similar education and experience so that if rejected by one candidate, they can draw new candidates from an ample labor pool.

Comparing Offers

The condition of the economy, the job seeker's academic major and particular geographic job market, and individual needs and demands for certain employment conditions may not provide more than one job offer at a time. Some job seekers may feel that no reasonable offer should go unaccepted for the simple fear there won't be another.

In a tough job market, or if the job you seek is not widely available, or when your job search goes on too long and becomes difficult to sustain financially and emotionally, it may be necessary to accept an inferior offer. The alternative is continued unemployment. Even here, when you feel you don't have a choice, you can at least understand that in accepting this particular offer, there may be limitations and conditions you don't appreciate. At the time of acceptance, there were no other alternatives, but you can begin to use that position to gain the experience and talent to move toward a more attractive position.

Sometimes, however, more than one offer is received, and the candidate has the luxury of choice. If the job seeker knows what he or she wants and has done the necessary self-assessment honestly and thoroughly, it may be clear that one of the offers conforms more closely to those expressed wants and needs.

However, if, as so often happens, the offers are similar in terms of conditions and salary, the question then becomes which organization might provide the necessary climate, opportunities, and advantages for your professional development and growth. This is the time when solid employer research and astute questioning during the interviews really pays off. How much did you learn about the employer through your own research and skillful questioning? When the interviewer asked during the interview "Do you have any questions?" did you ask the kinds of questions that would help resolve a choice between one organization and another? Just as an employer must decide among numerous applicants, so must the applicant learn to assess the potential employer. Both are partners in the job search.

Reneging on an Offer

An especially disturbing occurrence for employers and career counseling professionals is when a job seeker formally (either orally or by written contract) accepts employment with one organization and later reneges on the agreement and goes with another employer.

There are all kinds of rationalizations offered for this unethical behavior. None of them satisfies. The sad irony is that what the job seeker is willing to do to the employer—make a promise and then break it—he or she would be outraged to have done to him- or herself: have the job offer pulled. It is a very bad way to begin a career. It suggests the individual has not taken the time to do the necessary self-assessment and self-awareness exercises to think and judge critically. The new offer taken may, in fact, be no better or worse than the one refused. You should be aware that there have been incidents of legal action following job candidates' reneging on an offer. This adds a very sour note to what should be a harmonious beginning of a lifelong adventure.

8

The Graduate School Choice

The reasons for furthering one's education in graduate school can be as varied and unique as the individuals electing this course of action. Many continue their studies at an advanced level because they simply find it difficult to end the educational process. They love what they are learning and want to learn more and broaden their academic exploration.

Focusing on a particular subject—such as the impact of computer automation on an increasingly diverse workforce—and thinking, studying, researching, and writing critically on what others have discovered can provide excitement, challenge, and serious work. Some computer majors have enjoyed this aspect of their academic experience and want to continue that activity.

Other students pursue graduate study for purely practical reasons; they have examined employment prospects in their field of study and all indications suggest that a graduate degree is needed. For example, if you have earned a B.S. in computer programming as a stepping-stone to a career in upper-level management or systems analysis, going on for further training becomes mandatory. As a bachelor's-level computer major, you realize you might not be able to move into more managerial positions, which suggests that to be competitive, pursuing at least a master's degree is important. Alumni who work in the government, for nonprofits, or in private industry can be a good source to find out what degree level the different settings are hiring. Ask your college career office for some alumni names and give them a telephone call. Prepare some questions on specific job prospects in their field at each degree level. A thorough examination of the marketplace and talking to employers and professors will give you a sense of the scope of employment for a bachelor's, master's, or other related degree.

College teaching will require a master's degree or doctorate. The more senior executive positions in the career paths outlined in Part Two will require advanced training and perhaps a particular specialization in a subject area.

Consider Your Motives

The answer to the question of "Why graduate school?" is a personal one for each applicant. Nevertheless, it is important to consider your motives carefully. Graduate school involves additional time out of the employment market, a high level of critical evaluation, significant autonomy as you pursue your studies, and considerable financial expenditure. For some students in doctoral programs, there may be additional life choice issues, such as relationships, marriage, and parenthood, that may present real challenges while in a program of study. You would be well advised to consider the following questions as you think about your decision to continue your studies.

Are You Postponing Some Tough Decisions by Going to School?
Graduate school is not a place to go to avoid life's problems. There is intense competition for graduate school slots and for the fellowships, scholarships, and financial aid available. This competition means extensive interviewing, résumé submission, and essay writing that rivals corporate recruitment. Likewise, the graduate school process is a mentored one in which faculty stay aware of and involved in the academic progress of their students and continually challenge the quality of their work. Many graduate students are called upon to participate in teaching and professional writing and research as well.

In other words, this is no place to hide from the spotlight. Graduate students work very hard and much is demanded of them individually. If you elect to go to graduate school to avoid the stresses and strains of the "real world," you will find no safe place in higher academics. Vivid accounts, both fictional and nonfictional, have depicted quite accurately the personal and professional demands of graduate school work.

The selection of graduate studies as a career option should be a positive choice—something you *want* to do. It shouldn't be selected as an escape from other, less attractive or more challenging options, nor should it be selected as the option of last resort (i.e., "I can't do anything else; I'd better just stay in school."). If you're in some doubt about the strength of your reasoning about continuing in school, discuss the issues with a career counselor or a faculty member at your school. Together you can clarify your reasoning, and you'll get some sound feedback on what you're about to undertake.

On the other hand, staying on in graduate school because of a particularly poor employment market and a lack of jobs at entry-level positions has proven to be an effective "stalling" strategy. If you can afford it, pursuing a graduate degree immediately after your undergraduate education gives you a year or two to "wait out" a difficult economic climate, while at the same time acquiring a potentially valuable credential.

Have You Done Some "Hands-On" Reality Testing?

There are experiential options available to give some reality to your decision-making process about graduate school. Internships or work in the field can give you a good idea about employment demands, conditions, and atmosphere.

Computer science majors who hope to enhance their careers may find that attending graduate school is a viable choice. Publications such as the *Wall Street Journal* (careerjournal.com) often contain articles about graduate training for computer professionals.

Computer science majors who want to take their education to a higher level with an eye toward college teaching will find that some "hands-on" reality testing is vital. Ask your college professors about their own educational and career paths as well as what their job actually entails, such as the time they spend outside the classroom, in research activities, or in departmental meetings. Talking to people and asking questions are invaluable as exercises to help you better understand the objective of graduate school.

For computer science majors, the opportunity to do this kind of reality testing helps to identify what your real-world skills are and how they can be put to use. Internships and co-op experiences can speed up that process and prevent the frustrating and expensive process of investigation many graduates begin only after graduation.

Have You Compared Your Expectations of What Graduate School Will Do for You with What It Has Done for Alumni of the Program You're Considering?

Most colleges and universities perform some kind of postgraduate survey of their students to ascertain where they are employed, what additional education they have received, and what levels of salary they are enjoying. Ask to see this information either from the university you are considering applying to or from your own alma mater, especially if it has a similar graduate program. Such surveys often reveal surprises about occupational decisions, salaries, and work satisfaction. This information may affect your decision.

The value of self-assessment (the process of examining and making decisions about your own hierarchy of values and goals) is especially important in analyzing the desirability of possible career paths involving graduate education. Sometimes a job requiring advanced education seems to hold real promise but is disappointing in salary potential or number of opportunities available. Certainly it is better to research this information before embarking on a program of graduate studies. It may not change your mind about your decision, but by becoming better informed about your choice, you become better prepared for your future.

Have You Talked with People in Your Field to Explore What You Might Be Doing After Graduate School?

In pursuing your undergraduate degree, you will have come into contact with many individuals trained in the field you are considering. You might also have the opportunity to attend professional conferences, workshops, seminars, and job fairs where you can expand your network of contacts. Talk to them all! Find out about their individual career paths, discuss your own plans and hopes, get their feedback on the reality of your expectations, and heed their advice about your prospects. Each will have a unique tale to tell, and each will bring a different perspective on the current marketplace for the credentials you are seeking. Talking to enough people will make you an expert on what's out there.

Are You Excited by the Idea of Studying the Particular Field You Have in Mind?

This question may be the most important one of all. If you are going to spend several years in advanced study, perhaps engendering some debt or postponing some lifestyle decisions for an advanced degree, you simply ought to enjoy what you're doing. Examine your work in the discipline so far. Has it been fun? Have you found yourself exploring various paths of thought? Do you read in your area for fun? Do you enjoy talking about it, thinking about it, and sharing it with others? Advanced degrees often are the beginning of a lifetime's involvement with a particular subject. Choose carefully a field that will hold your interest and your enthusiasm.

If nothing else, do the following:

- Talk and question (remember to listen!)
- Reality test
- Soul-search by yourself or with a person you trust

Finding the Right Program for You: Some Considerations

There are several important factors in coming to a sound decision about the right graduate program for you. You'll want to begin by locating institutions that offer appropriate programs, examining each of these programs and their requirements, undertaking the application process by reviewing catalogs and obtaining application materials, visiting campuses if possible, arranging for letters of recommendation, writing your application statement, and, finally, following up on your applications.

Locate Institutions with Appropriate Programs

Once you decide on a particular advanced degree, it's important to develop a list of schools offering such a degree program. Perhaps the best source of graduate program information is Peterson's. The website (petersons.com) and the printed *Guides to Graduate Study* allow you to search for information by institution name, location, or academic area. The website also allows you to do a keyword search. Use the website and guides to build your list. In addition, you may want to consult the College Board's *Index of Majors and Graduate Degrees*, which will help you find graduate programs offering the degree you seek. It is indexed by academic major and then categorized by state.

Now, this may be a considerable list. You may want to narrow the choices down further by a number of criteria: tuition, availability of financial aid, public versus private institutions, United States versus international institutions, size of student body, size of faculty, application fee, and geographic location. This is only a partial list; you will have your own important considerations. Perhaps you are an avid scuba diver and you find it unrealistic to think you could pursue graduate study for a number of years without being able to ocean dive from time to time. Good! That's a decision and it's honest. Now, how far from the ocean is too far, and what schools meet your other needs? In any case, and according to your own criteria, begin to put together a reasonable list of graduate schools that you are willing to spend time investigating.

Examine the Degree Programs and Their Requirements

Once you've determined the criteria by which you want to develop a list of graduate schools, you can begin to examine the degree program requirements, faculty composition, and institutional research orientation. Again, using resources such as Peterson's website or guides can reveal an amazingly rich level of material by which to judge your possible selections.

In addition to degree programs and degree requirements, entries will include information about application fees, entrance test requirements, tuition, percentage of applicants accepted, numbers of applicants receiving financial aid, gender breakdown of students, numbers of full- and part-time faculty, and often gender breakdown of faculty as well. Numbers graduating in each program and research orientations of departments are also included in some entries. There is information on graduate housing; student services; and library, research, and computer facilities. A contact person, phone number, and address are also standard information in these listings.

It can be helpful to draw up a chart and enter relevant information about each school you are considering in order to have a ready reference on points of information that are important to you.

Undertake the Application Process

Program Information. Once you've decided on a selection of schools, obtain program information and applications. Nearly every school has a website that contains most of the detailed information you need to narrow your choices. In addition, applications can be printed from the site. If, however, you don't want to print out lots of information, you can request that a copy of the catalog and application materials be sent to you.

When you have your information in hand, give it all a careful reading and make notes of issues you might want to discuss via E-mail, on the telephone, or in a personal interview.

What is the ratio of faculty to the required number of courses for your degree? How often will you encounter the same faculty member as an instructor?

If the program offers a practicum or off-campus experience, who arranges this? Does the graduate school select a site and place you there, or is it your responsibility? What are the professional affiliations of the faculty? Does the program merit any outside professional endorsement or accreditation?

Critically evaluate the catalogs of each of the programs you are considering. List any questions you have and ask current or former teachers and colleagues for their impressions as well.

The Application. Preview each application thoroughly to determine what you need to provide in the way of letters of recommendation, transcripts from undergraduate schools or any previous graduate work, and personal essays. Make a notation for each application of what you will need to complete that document.

Additionally, you'll want to determine entrance testing requirements for each institution and immediately arrange to register for appropriate tests. Information can be obtained from associated websites, including ets.org (GRE, GMAT, TOEFL, PRAXIS, SLS, Higher Education Assessment), lsat .org (LSAT), and tpcweb.com/mat (MAT). Your college career office should also be able to provide you with advice and additional information.

Visit the Campus if Possible

If time and finances allow, a visit, interview, and tour can help make your decision easier. You can develop a sense of the student body, meet some of the faculty, and hear up-to-date information on resources and the curriculum. You will have a brief opportunity to "try out" the surroundings to see if they fit your needs. After all, it will be home for a while. If a visit is not possible but you have questions, don't hesitate to call and speak with the dean of the graduate school. Most are more than happy to talk to candidates and want them to have the answers they seek. Graduate school admission is a very personal and individual process.

Arrange for Letters of Recommendation

This is also the time to begin to assemble a group of individuals who will support your candidacy as a graduate student by writing letters of recommendation or completing recommendation forms. Some schools will ask you to provide letters of recommendation to be included with your application or sent directly to the school by the recommender. Other graduate programs will provide a recommendation form that must be completed by the recommender. These graduate school forms vary greatly in the amount of space provided for a written recommendation. So that you can use letters as you need to, ask your recommenders to address their letters "To Whom It May Concern," unless one of your recommenders has a particular connection to one of your graduate schools or knows an official at the school.

Choose recommenders who can speak authoritatively about the criteria important to selection officials at your graduate school. In other words, choose recommenders who can write about your grasp of the literature in your field of study, your ability to write and speak effectively, your class performance, and your demonstrated interest in the field outside of class. Other characteristics that graduate schools are interested in assessing include your emotional maturity, leadership ability, breadth of general knowledge, intellectual ability, motivation, perseverance, and ability to engage in independent inquiry.

When requesting recommendations, it's especially helpful to put the request in writing. Explain your graduate school intentions and express some of your thoughts about graduate school and your appreciation for their support. Don't be shy about "prompting" your recommenders with some suggestions of what you would appreciate being included in their comments. Most recommenders will find this direction helpful and will want to produce a statement of support that you can both stand behind. Consequently, if your interaction with one recommender was especially focused on research projects, he or she might be best able to speak of those skills and your critical thinking ability. Another recommender may have good comments to make about your public presentation skills.

Give your recommenders plenty of lead time in which to complete your recommendation, and set a date by which they should respond. If they fail to meet your deadline, be prepared to make a polite call or visit to inquire if they need more information or if there is anything you can do to move the process along.

Whether you are providing a graduate school form or asking for an original letter to be mailed, be sure to provide an envelope and postage if the recommender must mail the form or letter directly to the graduate school.

Each recommendation you request should provide a different piece of information about you for the selection committee. It might be pleasant for letters of recommendation to say that you are a fine, upstanding individual, but a selection committee for graduate school will require specific information. Each recommender has had a unique relationship with you, and his or her letter should reflect that. Think of each letter as helping to build a more complete portrait of you as a potential graduate student.

Write Your Application Statement

The application and personal essay should be a welcome opportunity for the computer science major to express his or her deep interest in pursuing graduate study. Your understanding of the challenges ahead, your commitment to the work involved, and your expressed self-awareness will weigh heavily in the decision process of the graduate school admissions committee.

An excellent source to help in writing this essay is *How to Write a Winning Personal Statement for Graduate and Professional School,* by Richard J. Stelzer. It has been written from the perspective of what graduate school selection committees are looking for when they read these essays. It provides helpful tips to keep your essay targeted on the kinds of issues and criteria that are important to selection committees and that provide them with the kind of information they can best utilize in making their decision.

Follow Up on Your Applications

After you have finished each application and mailed it along with your transcript requests and letters of recommendation, be sure to follow up on the progress of your file. For example, call the graduate school administrative staff to see whether your transcripts have arrived. If the school required your recommenders to fill out a specific recommendation form that had to be mailed directly to the school, you will want to ensure that they have all arrived in good time for the processing of your application. It is your responsibility to make certain that all required information is received by the institution.

Researching Financial Aid Sources, Scholarships, and Fellowships

Financial aid information is available from the academic department to which you apply and from the university's graduate school. Some disciplines provide full tuition and a monthly stipend for graduate students. These decisions are made in the specific academic department. It is important that you ask about the availability of this type of financial support. If it is not available, you may be eligible for federal, state, and/or institutional support. There are lengthy forms to complete, and some of these will vary by school, type of school (public versus private), and state. Be sure to note the deadline dates on each form.

There are many excellent resources available to help you explore all of your financial aid options. Visit your college career office or local public library to find out about the range of materials available. Two excellent resources are Peterson's website (petersons.com) and its book *Peterson's Grants for Graduate and Post Doctoral Study.* Another good reference is the Foundation Center's *Foundation Grants to Individuals.* These types of resources generally contain information that can be accessed by indexes including field of study, specific eligibility requirements, administering agency, and geographic focus.

Evaluating Acceptances

If you apply to and are accepted at more than one school, it is time to return to your initial research and self-assessment to evaluate your options and select the program that will best help you achieve the goals you set for pursuing graduate study. You'll want to choose a program that will allow you to complete your studies in a timely and cost-effective way. This may be a good time to get additional feedback from professors and career professionals who are familiar with your interests and plans. Ultimately, the decision is yours, so be sure you get answers to all the questions you can think of.

Some Notes About Rejection

Each graduate school is searching for applicants who appear to have the qualifications necessary to succeed in its program. Applications are evaluated on a combination of undergraduate grade point average, strength of letters of recommendation, standardized test scores, and personal statements written for the application.

A carelessly completed application is one reason many applicants are denied admission to a graduate program. To avoid this type of needless rejection, be sure to carefully and completely answer all appropriate questions on the application form, focus your personal statement given the instructions provided, and submit your materials well in advance of the deadline. Remember that your test scores and recommendations are considered a part of your application, so they must also be received by the deadline.

If you are rejected by a school that especially interests you, you may want to contact the dean of graduate studies to discuss the strengths and weaknesses of your application. Information provided by the dean will be useful in reapplying to the program later or applying to other, similar programs.

PART TWO

THE CAREER PATHS

9

Introduction to the Computer Science Career Paths

"Technology improves things so fast that, by the time we can afford the best, there's something better."
—ANONYMOUS

Very few aspects of everyday life have been left untouched by the computer revolution. When you buy something at the store, most likely your purchase will be scanned at the checkout counter by a UPC bar code scanner. Bring a package to your local post office to mail, and the clerk will put it on a scale that is attached to a computer terminal. After the clerk inputs some information by pressing a few buttons, the computer's display tells you exactly how much the package will cost to mail. CAT scans help doctors view kidneys, hearts, and other body organs to see if they are healthy. Farmers rely on computers to plan planting and harvesting of crops. Every time you reserve space on an airplane, check your bank statement, or phone a friend, you are depending on computers.

With this tremendous growth has come an accompanying demand for personnel in the computer industry—all types at all levels, but for the most part, people skilled in computer science—to handle jobs both within and outside the industry. People are needed to handle such tasks as design and engineering of computer hardware and software, and in sales and service, systems development and programming, and computer operations.

In recent years, the use of sophisticated technology has become commonplace in all types of organizations. Large corporations, midsize businesses, colleges and universities, hospitals, government agencies, and other organizations all depend on computer technology to conduct core operations. Internal computer networks are commonplace, as are those joining more distant locations. A continuing demand exists for computer professionals trained to design and use computer equipment, ranging from mainframe computers to networked personal computers.

The rapid growth of the Internet as a business medium also bodes well for those interested in computer science careers. Electronic commerce is no longer in its infancy, and more and more business is now being conducted via the World Wide Web or other avenues for electronic communication. Conducting such business involves a variety of functions, from designing and maintaining web pages to developing and managing extensive databases used to store information on customers, sales, logistics, and other important topics. To meet the need for these functions, twenty-first century employers must retain personnel who are skilled in various applications of information technology.

Of course, accurately predicting the future is impossible, but we do know that, whatever the next few decades bring, computer technology will be right in the center of things. As computer technology continues to advance and develop for both home and industry, there will be an ever-growing need for computer professionals to fill the ensuing job openings. Career opportunities in the computer field will remain strong, and knowledge of computer technology will continue to become more and more important to workers in every field.

Career paths in computer-related fields are as diverse as the applications of computer technology. A vast number of avenues are open to computer science graduates, and it's hard to know where to begin in describing them. This book is designed to help you sort out your options in order to make an intelligent decision about your future.

In This Book

Though this book does not provide information about every career in the world of computer science, the chapters that follow offer an abundance of information about many careers in this field. Though there are overlapping duties and responsibilities for those who perform many of the jobs, people in this field all have one element in common—a love for solving problems and making life better through the use of computers.

The six career paths described in this book follow:

- **Path 1. Computer Scientists and Systems Analysts.** This chapter provides an in-depth look at the work done by systems analysts and related computer professionals. It focuses on opportunities for those who design and develop new hardware or software systems, incorporate new technologies, administer databases, and solve computer problems, among other tasks.

- **Path 2. Management Analysts and Consultants.** Those with a business background may find this chapter particularly interesting. It covers careers involving the application of management techniques to solve business problems and foster improvement in areas such as organizational structure, business communication, and productivity.
- **Path 3. Operations Research Analysts.** Specialized careers in operations research are the focus of this chapter. Readers with strong quantitative skills and a penchant for detailed analysis may find this section of special interest.
- **Path 4. Computer Operators and Programmers.** This chapter covers occupations involving the direct operation of computers, the development and revision of software, and related areas.
- **Path 5. Computer Sales and Service.** Careers related to selling, installing, repairing, or maintaining computer equipment are reviewed in this chapter. It includes a look at a variety of positions, ranging from computer technicians to sales professionals.
- **Path 6. Other Computer Science Careers.** Here, a number of other careers are explored. You'll find information on such diverse areas as teaching, systems integration, data entry, and technical writing.

Computer science is a vast field that provides many opportunities for those who are willing to prepare themselves and work hard to achieve success. Read on to determine which area of computer science appeals to you most, and then take the necessary steps to fulfill your dream.

> *"Far and away the best prize that life offers is the chance to work hard at work worth doing."*
> —THEODORE ROOSEVELT

10

Path 1:
Computer Scientists and
Systems Analysts

"Computers are useless. They can only give you answers."
—PABLO PICASSO

Help Wanted: Computer Scientists and Engineers. We are a high-technology company specializing in state-of-the-art software engineering and computer services. We are seeking high-quality computer scientists and engineers for our southwest Washington location. Bachelor of science degree in engineering, computer science, or a related field. Excellent benefits/relocation package.

Requires any of the following knowledge areas/skills:

MS Access

SQL

FileMaker

Oracle

C/C++

Assembler

CICS

Must be U.S. citizen and meet eligibility requirements for access to classified information. We are a drug-free workplace. Send résumé with salary requirements in strictest confidence.

This is a typical ad you might expect to find in a city newspaper. It is genuine, as are all of the want ads in this book. Each one provides insights into the kinds of professionals employers are seeking and also reveals information about qualifications, work expectations, and compensation. The want ads allow you to peek into the world of computers. Perhaps you will decide that it is the world you will choose to make your career.

Definition of the Career Path

Computers—it's hard to imagine a world without them. As a result of new technologies, particularly in the past twenty years or so, our modern society has been deluged by a continual introduction of new products, both in computer hardware systems and software.

The manufacturing of computer hardware includes all the components, such as the central processing unit (CPU), and peripheral equipment, such as disks, monitors, storage devices, tape drives, and printers.

Computer software consists of one or more programs made up of machine-readable instructions that perform a logical sequence of functions—anything from maintaining a bookkeeping system to performing computer games.

All of the remarkable and continuing advances in computer technology may be credited to the highly trained and skilled group of professionals called computer scientists, which includes computer designers, software designers, computer engineers, product designers, systems analysts, computer support analysts, and database managers and administrators.

Computer Scientist

Computer scientists conduct research, design computers, and discover and use principles of applied computer technology. Though they may perform many of the same duties as other computer professionals, their jobs are distinguished by the higher level of theoretical expertise they apply to complex problems and the innovative ideas necessary for the application or creation of new technology.

Computer professionals who are employed by academic institutions work in areas from theory, to hardware, to language design, or to multidisciplinary projects (for example, developing and advancing uses for artificial intelligence. Their counterparts in private industry work in areas such as applying theory; developing specialized languages; or designing programming tools, knowledge-based systems, or computer games.

Computer Designer

Designers in the computer industry are responsible for researching and developing new computer hardware products. They analyze data to determine the feasibility of a product, work with other research personnel to develop a detailed description of the product, and plan and develop experimental test programs to determine the success or failure of their designs.

Computer Product Design Engineer

Computer product design engineers work with designers. Together they are responsible for developing new computer hardware products.

Computer engineers concentrate on the hardware and software aspects of systems design and development, assist designers in the development of specifications, and supervise other engineers. They often work as part of a team that designs new computing devices or computer-related equipment.

Software Engineer

Software engineers focus their efforts on maintaining, enhancing, and/or debugging existing software. They may also be responsible for the proper operation of computer systems and create new software programs.

> **Help Wanted: Software Engineer.** National specialty managed-care company seeking an individual with a strong technical background in client/server application coding and database administration and design. The qualified individual should have a bachelor's degree in computer science or a related field, a minimum of three years' experience using SQL Windows and C++, and working with a relational database.

Software Developer

Software developers produce computer-based products (both packaged and systems software) and services for both individual consumers and corpora-

> **Help Wanted: Software Application Developers.** Responsibilities include developing our next generation of Manufacturing Application Software. Duties will include the design and development of enhanced requirements, planning, and scheduling software products in a client/server environment.
>
> Requirements include a bachelor's degree or equivalent experience, strong C++ programming skills, and manufacturing software development experience, particularly MRP or Production Scheduling. Preference will be given to candidates with experience in Optimization, Finite Capacity Scheduling, or Constraining-Based Planning/Scheduling. Memory Resident Programming experience and/or CASE tool knowledge is also a plus.

tions. They coordinate the production of software products, from choosing content providers, assembling graphics creators, and working with programmers, through the actual assembling, pressing, and distribution of the end product. Much of a software developer's day is spent on the telephone in an attempt to coordinate the production of software products with other members of the working team. These professionals report that there is a feeling of pride in creating something that previously didn't exist.

Software Designer

Software designers are the researchers who create the operating systems that allow users to interface with the computer. In addition, they create the software products that perform specific functions or applications such as word-processing packages.

Software designers assess needs, create a chart showing how the program will work, and determine the components that will appear on each screen. Then, based on the customer's existing equipment or preferences, they devise compatible software. Software designers also update, debug, and modify existing programs.

Help Wanted: Software Design Engineer. Our company is growing—come join the team!

Design, develop, and implement software for Real Time Operating Systems. Qualified candidates will have a bachelor of science degree in computer science or a related field and experience with Real Time Operating Systems, Developing Communications Protocols, and Operating Systems (C, C++ preferred).

We are a high-technology electronic engineering designer of real time single board computers. End users of our products require flexible capability, exceptional reliability, high-speed processing capacity, and deterministic computer response time, particularly in communications applications. Excellent benefits and casual work environment.

Computer Database Manager and Administrator

Computer database managers and database administrators design, write, and oversee computer database systems in an effort to make sure that the right person can access the right information at the right time. Their main responsibilities include maintaining the efficiency of the database, in addition to the following:

1. Organizing the information into a computer file
2. Watching over the system to make sure that users do not tamper with the information or the system structure (the way it is put together)
3. Making or approving all changes or modifications to the database information or program

Computer database managers and administrators may also be responsible for maintaining the security of their systems.

Computer Support Analyst

Computer support analysts are responsible for providing assistance and advice to users; interpreting problems; and providing technical support for hardware, software, and systems. They may be employed by organizations or computer or software vendors.

Help Wanted: Systems Analyst. Our state university invites nominations and applications for a systems analyst position. This position is an outstanding opportunity for the highly motivated, serious programmer desiring experience with exciting technology. A bachelor's degree in computer science or related field from a regionally accredited institution is required. Professional experience in object-oriented programming and SQL applications is preferred. Professional programming experience in an IBM/MVS mainframe environment is required. Experience with Internet and/or webserver development, SQL, JavaScript, HTML, XML required. Familiarity with application servers WebSphere 4.0, Web Servers IBM HTTP also desired.

This position provides the opportunity to work with the latest technologies. Assignments may include projects such as developing and/or installing and maintaining client/server application systems for the university library, providing SQL applications and reports for administrative departments, or developing mainframe solutions in existing administrative systems. Interpersonal relationship skills are essential to work with and train administrative users. The systems analyst will receive assignments and technical supervision from the administrative programming manager.

Applications must include a letter that specifically addresses how skills, education, and experience relate to the position announcement. Also, include a résumé and a list of three references.

About 400,000 people are employed as systems analysts—professionals who are hired to define business, scientific, or engineering problems and design their solutions using computers. Systems analysts may design entirely new systems, including hardware and software, or add a single new software application to harness more of the computer's power.

As architects of the computer team, systems analysts begin their work by meeting with various persons who are involved in the project. For instance, the Internal Revenue Service might seek a new system designed to process tax returns, but the auditors and accountants don't know how to set this up, so they will seek the aid of a systems analyst.

Much time is devoted to clearly defining the goals of the system so that it can be broken down into separate programmable procedures. Through the use of techniques such as structured analysis, data modeling, information engineering, and cost accounting, systems analysts map out the new system. Once the design has been developed, systems analysts prepare charts and diagrams that describe the system in terms that managers and other users can understand. Following this, systems analysts often prepare a cost-benefit and return-on-investment analysis to help management decide whether the proposed system will be satisfactory to meet their needs.

After this study is completed, analysts translate the requirements of the existing system into the capabilities of a computer system. They then prepare specifications for programmers to follow so that the programmers can accurately write the programs necessary to make the computer system function as required.

Some organizations do not employ programmers; instead, a single worker, called a programmer/analyst, is responsible for both systems analysis and programming.

Help Wanted: Programmer/Systems Analyst. Our manufacturing company with multiple locations is upgrading to a UNIX environment, using HP hardware and operating system. We will also be implementing the MFG/PRO and Progress software business system. To facilitate this growth, we are currently seeking a programmer/systems analyst.

The ideal candidate will have a bachelor's degree, knowledge of HP hardware and operating systems, and two years' programming experience using Progress software. Experience with Word, Excel, and other Microsoft products required. Current certified Novell administrator is preferred, with EDI and/or bar code experience a plus. In return, we offer a comprehensive compensation and benefits package.

Some analysts become involved with every conceivable type of system. A business systems analyst may work with accounts receivable, accounts payable, inventory, general ledger, payroll, or any other type of business system. A scientific or engineering systems analyst may work for NASA, for example, on a system that analyzes stresses on steel beams or a system that is designed to send a man or woman to the moon.

Because up-to-date information—accounting records, sales figures, or budget projections, for example—is so important in modern organizations, systems analysts may be instructed to make the computer systems in each department compatible with one another so that facts and figures can be shared. Similarly, electronic mail requires open pathways to send messages, documents, and data from one computer "mailbox" to another across different equipment and program lines. Analysts must design the hardware and software to allow free exchange of data, custom applications, and the computer power to process it all. They study the seemingly incompatible pieces and create ways to link them so that users can access information from any part of the system.

Possible Job Titles

Computer database administrator
Computer database manager
Computer designer
Computer engineer
Computer product design engineer
Computer scientist
Computer support analyst

Internet developer
Software applications developer
Software designer
Software developer
Software engineer
Systems analyst

Possible Employers

At present, about 887,000 professionals are employed as computer scientists, systems analysts, and database administrators. Although they can be found in small offices and most industries (manufacturing, banking, hospitals, travel, and hospitality, for example), the greatest concentration is in the computer and data-processing services industry. This includes firms that design and install computer systems, integrate or network systems, perform data processing and database management, develop packaged software, and even

Help Wanted: Systems Analysts. Make the most of your talent by joining our team!

Knowledgeable? Energetic? Are you looking for a challenging position that opens up a world of career opportunities? These are the kinds of people we are searching for to join our team. We want you to help us in developing mission-critical solutions using state-of-the-art technology, while making the most of your skills and broadening your expertise.

As a systems analyst you will help define user requirements and systems specifications for manufacturing, distribution, and retail financial applications. To qualify, you must have at least five years of IS (Information Systems) experience, which should include prior programming and development experience, as well as exposure to entity, data, and process modeling. Strong platform and workshop facilitation skills are preferred, along with broad-based knowledge of business operations.

operate entire computer facilities under contract. Many others work for government agencies (particularly in the armed forces), for manufacturers of computers and related electronic equipment, for insurance companies, and for universities.

A growing number of computer scientists and systems analysts are employed on a temporary or contract basis. For example, a company installing a new computer system may need the services of several systems analysts to get their systems up and running, but these professionals would only be needed temporarily. Such jobs may last from several months to two years or more.

Related Occupations

Other workers who use research, logic, and creativity to solve business problems are listed:

Actuary

Computer programmer

Consultant

Electronic publishing professional

Engineer

Financial analyst

Management analyst

Manager

Manufacturing and product development professional

Operations research analyst

Professional involved in translation services for annual reports

Programmer

Urban planner

> **Help Wanted: Systems Analyst.** Your solid background in hands-on application development, combined with good communications and interpersonal skills, will allow you to excel in technical projects, with possibilities for eventual advancement to a leadership role. Requires solid problem-solving, writing, and organizational skills to supplement technical expertise in a variety of software packages. Insurance industry knowledge or background is highly desired.

Working Conditions

Computer scientists and systems analysts usually enjoy a pleasant working environment in comfortable surroundings in offices or laboratories amid state-of-the-art equipment. Given the technology available today, more work, including technical support, can be done from remote locations using modems, laptops, electronic mail, and even through the Internet.

These technical professionals usually work independently, about forty hours a week, the same as many other professional or office workers. Occasionally projects may pile up, however, dictating the necessity of working evening or weekend hours to meet deadlines or solve problems. Travel may also be a prominent part of the job and should be considered a definite possibility.

Because computer scientists and systems analysts spend long periods in front of a computer terminal typing on a keyboard, they are susceptible to eyestrain, back discomfort, and hand and wrist problems.

Training and Qualifications

College graduates are almost always sought for computer professional positions, and, for some of the more complex jobs, persons with graduate degrees are preferred. Generally a computer scientist working in a research lab or academic institution will hold a Ph.D. or master's degree in computer science or engineering. Some computer scientists are able to gain sufficient experience for this type of position with only a bachelor's degree, but this is more difficult. Computer engineers generally have a bachelor's degree in computer engineering, electrical engineering, or mathematics. Computer designers need a minimum of a bachelor's degree in computer science or engineering. However, a master's degree is preferred.

Computer product design engineers are required to have a bachelor's degree in computer science or engineering. At one time, software designers were required to have a bachelor's or master's degree in computer science. But now experience may be given a considerable amount of weight also.

Software developers need to be flexible and organized, have strong interpersonal and technical skills, and have a high tolerance for failure and frustration. Professionals must be self-starters who can tackle problems head-on.

Software designers need to have a solid understanding of various program languages and must work diligently to keep up with changes in their field. They also need skill in working with computer hardware and peripherals.

For database managers or administrators, a doctoral degree in computer science or advanced courses in computer programming may be required, along with courses in business management and computer science. At lower positions, an associate's degree may be sufficient. Professionals in this field need to be skilled at managing databases and people.

The Institute for Certification of Computer Professionals offers the designation certified computing professional (CCP) to those who have four years of experience and who pass a core examination, plus exams in two specialty areas. Core exams are available in the following areas: microcomputers and networks, procedural programming, software engineering, systems programming, data resource management, management, business information systems, office information systems, systems development, communications, and systems security. The Quality Assurance Institute awards the designation certified quality analyst (CQA) to those who meet education and experience requirements, pass an exam, and endorse a code of ethics. Neither designation is mandatory, but either may provide a job seeker a competitive advantage.

Computer support analysts may also need a bachelor's degree in a computer-related field, as well as significant experience working with computers, including programming skills.

Georgia State University, which offers a bachelor of science degree in computer science, offers the following information about its program, which is not unlike many programs of this type offered by colleges and universities throughout the United States and Canada.

Georgia State's B.S. program provides preparation in the fundamental principles and processes of computation and the basic mathematics and physics on which these principles and processes depend. The program also provides for the application of these principles to problems in the area of business.

Basic requirements include a minimum grade of "C" in all mathematics and computer science courses and all upper-level courses that are required in the undergraduate programs of this department. In addition, for the programs following, the total of 120 hours must include at least 45 hours of upper-division courses numbered 3000 or above.

Courses required for the major include those from the undergraduate core curriculum (areas A–E as noted), courses appropriate to the major (area F), major courses (area G), and minor and additional courses (area H). The number of credit hours is indicated in parentheses. Students must receive credit for the calculus courses Math 2211, 2212, and 2215; the discrete mathematics course Math 2420; and the introductory computer science courses Computer Science 2010 and 2310 in the core curriculum areas A–F.

- Area A: Essential Skills (9). Required course: Math 1113 Pre-calculus (or a higher level mathematics course) (3)
- Area B: Institutional Options (4)
- Area C: Humanities and Fine Arts (6)
- Area D: Science, Mathematics, and Technology (11). Required courses: Math 2211 Calculus of One Variable I (or a higher level mathematics course) (4). Physics 2211K and 2212K, Principles of Physics I and II (4 each)
- Area E: Social Science (12)
- Area F: Courses Appropriate to the Major Field (18)

1. Required course(s): selected from course(s) not taken in Area A or D (0–16)
   Math 2212 Calculus of One Variable II (4)
   Math 2215 Multivariate Calculus (4)
   Physics 2211K Principles of Physics I (4) if not taken in Area D
   Physics 2212K Principles of Physics II (4) if not taken in Area D
2. Additional courses consisting of 18 hours in Area F (0–18)
   Accounting 2101, Accounting 2102
   Biology 1107K, Biology 1108K
   Chemistry 1211K, Chemistry 1212K
   Chemistry 2400
   Computer Science 2010
   Computer Science 2301
   Computer Science 2310, Computer Science 2311
   Economics 2105, Economics 2106
   Foreign Language 2001, Foreign Language 2002
   Latin 2002

Math 2420
Philosophy 2410, Philosophy 2420

- Area G: Major Requirements (48)

1. In addition to the courses placed in the core curriculum, such as
   Physics 2211K and 2212K, all computer science majors must
   complete Math 3030 (Mathematical Models for Computer Science)
   and Physics 3500 (Electronics) (6).
2. Computer Science Requirements (27)
   Computer Science 2311 Principles of Programming II (3)
   Computer Science 3210 Computer Organization and
      Programming (3)
   Computer Science 3320 System-Level Programming (3)
   Computer Science 3410 Data Structures (3)
   Computer Science 4210 Computer Architecture (3)
   Computer Science 4330 Programming Language Concepts (3)
   Computer Science 4350 Software Engineering (3)
   Computer Science 4520 Design and Analysis of Algorithms (3)
   Computer Science 4610 Numerical Analysis I (3)
3. One course selected from the following (3):
   Computer Science 4220 Computer Networks (3)
   Computer Science 4310 Introduction to Parallel Programming (3)
   Computer Science 4320 Operating Systems (3)
4. Four courses from those following and those not taken in area 3
   preceding (12):
   Computer Science 3360 Windowing Systems Programming (3)
   Computer Science 4340 Introduction to Compilers (3)
   Computer Science 4510 Automata (3)
   Computer Science 4620 Numerical Analysis II (3)
   Computer Science 4710 Database Systems (3)
   Computer Science 4720 Human–Computer Interaction (3)
   Computer Science 4730 Scientific Visualization (3)
   Computer Science 4810 Artificial Intelligence (3)
   Computer Science 4820 Computer Graphics Algorithms (3)
   Computer Science 4830 System Simulation (3)
   Others approved by the department
5. Additional Courses (12)
   Four additional courses as electives (12)

- Area H: Minor and Additional Courses

1. Students earning a B.S. in the Department of Computer Science are not required to complete a minor.
2. Additional courses must be taken as electives to complete a minimum of 120 semester hours, exclusive of 1000/2000 physical education or military science courses.

Residency Requirement: Degree candidates must earn 39 semester hours at Georgia State University in courses at the 3000 level or above, with an average grade of "C" or better. At least one-half of the courses comprising the major or 11 semester hours in the major, whichever is less, must be taken at Georgia State University.

Qualifications for Systems Analysts

For a business environment, employers usually want systems analysts to have a background in business management or a closely related field. For scientifically oriented organizations, a background in the physical sciences, applied mathematics, or engineering is preferred. Many employers seek applicants who have a bachelor's degree in computer science, information science, computer information systems, or data processing. Regardless of the college major, employers look for people who are familiar with programming languages and have a broad knowledge of computer systems and technologies.

To achieve the title of systems analyst, one must have years of experience in data processing. This job experience is necessary for the analyst to fully comprehend the system being studied.

Systems analysts must be able to think logically, have good communication skills, and like working with people and ideas. They often deal with a number of tasks simultaneously. The ability to concentrate and pay close attention to detail also is important. Although systems analysts often work independently, they also work in teams on large projects. They must be able to communicate effectively with technical personnel, such as programmers and managers, as well as with other staff who may have no technical computer background.

Professionals with the title of systems analysts may be promoted to senior or lead systems analysts after gaining several years of experience. Those who show leadership abilities may advance to management positions, such as manager of information systems or chief information officer.

Help Wanted: Systems Analyst. Our university is seeking a systems analyst. The successful candidate will provide system support, training, reporting, troubleshooting, and maintenance for mainframe, network, and PC systems and files for enrollment management at the school. In addition, responsibilities include working with vendors regarding interface and data transmissions. To qualify, you must possess a bachelor's degree with experience in programming and/or systems analysis. Excellent interpersonal and organizational skills required. Preferred candidates will have mainframe programming and/or analysis background and familiarity with CICS and COBOL. Expertise in network and/or PC operations and/or experience with student information systems a plus.

Many people develop advanced computer skills in other occupations, in which they work extensively with computers and then transfer into computer occupations. For example, an accountant may become a systems analyst specializing in accounting systems development, or a person may move into a systems analyst job after working as a computer programmer.

Earnings

According to the *Occupational Outlook Handbook* (*OOH*), prepared by the U.S. Department of Labor, the median annual earnings of computer systems analysts and scientists who work full-time is about $59,300. The middle 50 percent earn between $46,980 and $73,210. The lowest 10 percent earn less than $37,460, and the highest 10 percent, more than $89,040.

Earnings for all computer scientists will vary according to the location, type of business, and size of the operation. Most positions offer paid holidays and vacations, along with health insurance and sick leave.

According to Robert Half International Inc., starting salaries for database administrators range from $72,500 to $105,750. In the federal government, the median annual salary for systems analysts is more than $59,000. For all employers, the average starting salary for graduates with a master's degree in computer science is more than $61,400, according to the National Association of Colleges and Employers.

Career Outlook

The *OOH* predicts that computer scientists and systems analysts will be among the fastest-growing occupations through the year 2010. In addition, tens of thousands of job openings will result annually from the need to replace workers who move into managerial positions or other occupations or who leave the labor force.

The demand for computer scientists and engineers is expected to rise as organizations attempt to maximize the efficiency of their computer systems. There will continue to be a need for increasingly sophisticated technological innovation. Competition will place organizations under growing pressure to use technological advances in areas such as office and factory automation, telecommunications technology, and scientific research. As the complexity of these applications grows, more computer scientists and systems analysts will be needed to design, develop, and implement the new technology.

As more computing power is made available to the individual user, more computer scientists and systems analysts will be required to provide support. As users develop more sophisticated knowledge of computers, they become more aware of the machine's potential and better able to suggest how computers could be used to increase their own productivity and that of the organization. Increasingly, users are able to design and implement more of their own applications and programs. As technology continues to advance, computer scientists and systems analysts will continue to need to upgrade their levels of skill and technical expertise, and their ability to interact with users will increase in importance.

The demand for "networking" to facilitate the sharing of information will be a major factor in the rising demand for systems analysts. Falling prices of computer hardware and software should continue to induce more small businesses to computerize their operations, further stimulating demand for these workers. To maintain a competitive edge and operate more cost effectively, firms will continue to demand computer professionals who are knowledgeable about the latest technologies and able to apply them to meet the needs of businesses. A greater emphasis on problem solving, analysis, and client/server environments will also contribute to the growing demand for systems analysts.

Strategy for Finding the Jobs

Persons with an advanced degree in computer science should enjoy very favorable employment prospects because employers are demanding a higher level of technical expertise. College graduates with a bachelor's degree in computer science, computer engineering, information science, or information systems should experience good prospects for employment. College graduates with noncomputer science majors who have had courses in computer programming, systems analysis, and other data-processing areas, as well as training or experience in an applied field, may also be able to find jobs as computer professionals. Those who are familiar with CASE tools, object-oriented and client/server programming, and multimedia technology will have an even greater advantage, as will persons with significant networking, database, and systems experience.

Campus employment service is still the best place for graduates to begin to seek job positions. Often, potential employers come to campuses to look for and interview potential candidates. Technical job fairs (both on and off campus) are also possibilities for potential employment. Want ads (similar to those included in this book) may be found in any newspaper, particularly the Sunday edition as well as on websites. Because virtually any company may avail itself of the services of computer scientists, there is a potential to land a job almost anywhere. Networking techniques are very important, as are other avenues such as joining professional associations; volunteering to help in a local, school, or community project; and seeking the aid of mentors.

Professional Associations

American Electronics Association
5201 Great America Pkwy.
P.O. Box 54990
Santa Clara, CA 95056-0990
aeanet.org

American Society for Information Science and Technology
1320 Fenwick Ln., Suite 510
Silver Spring, MD 20910
asis.org

Association for Computing Machinery
One Astor Plaza
1515 Broadway
New York, NY 10036-5701
acm.org

Association for Women in Computing
41 Sutter St., Suite 1006
San Francisco, CA 94104
awc-hq.org

IEEE Computer Society
Headquarters Office
1730 Massachusetts Ave. NW
Washington, DC 20036-1992
computer.org

Institute for Certification of Computing Professionals
2350 E. Devon Ave., Suite 115
Des Plaines, IL 60018-4610
iccp.org/iccpnew/index.html

Meet Ron Burris

Ron Burris earned an associate in arts degree through Allan Hancock College, an associate in science degree through the Ground Wire Communications Technology program of the Community College of the Air Force, and also attended the computer programming technical school in Biloxi, Mississippi, in addition to completing some classes at San Diego State University. He has extensive experience in hardware and software programs, software development, systems analysis network design, end-user support and education, project planning, accounting and management, technical and proposal writing, retail and consulting business operations, management and telephone plant installation, maintenance operations, and management. He has served as a software engineer, technical writer, programmer/analyst, and consultant.

"I began as a hobbyist in 1975," says Burris. "Subsequently, I entered the computer field professionally in 1978, when I started writing articles for *Kilobaud* magazine (the second national microcomputer magazine—*Byte* was first). I've always been technically inclined," he says, "building radios, electronic test equipment, and so forth since I was in grammar school.

"After private contract consulting for several years, I took a job designing and programming software for my present employer, a pharmaceutical claims processor. It's a small company, thirty-five employees, with four in the computer services department. The atmosphere is fairly casual, though the pace is hectic. We're maintaining an inadequately written software system while designing, building, and implementing replacement software. Because of constantly changing requirements from and for our clients, we do a lot of 'batch and patch' programming to keep the revenue flowing while we work toward an elegant solution. The hours per week vary from about thirty to about fifty, depending on what's going on.

"I like the autonomy of this position," Burris says. "My supervisor allows me the flexibility to get the job done on my terms, as long as it's done well. My least favorite thing is being interrupted in my work to fix someone else's computer—usually simple stuff they could do themselves. On the other hand, I am paid well, receive a good benefits package, and work close to home. On the downside is the fact that prior management bought overly cheap equipment and hired programmers who didn't believe in using database software to maintain databases, which makes the code tracing to fix a simple problem a nightmare.

"I would advise others to live long and prosper—keep up on current technology and avoid following the fads."

Meet Steve Pflug

Steve Pflug's work experience includes service as a network administrator, as well as a technician providing PC support. He attended DeVry Technical Institute in Kansas City and received a bachelor of arts degree in telecommunications management. His previous experience includes PC support and networking.

"I entered the computer field via the air force," Pflug says. "As a network administrator, 75 percent of a typical day is spent fielding service requests, mainly printer-related problems. I spend most of the remaining 25 percent dealing with user problems. I also take some time to customize service reports and forms for people. Somehow every day, I also sandwich in reviewing and reading about the software the company uses. I feel that it's important to keep up with the latest technology.

"Our work atmosphere is very relaxed and laid back," he says. "I usually work an average of fifty hours per week, including some evenings and weekends. The hectic time is during implementation of new software and upgrades.

"To succeed in a position such as this, you need minor programming skills; networking and topography background; good knowledge of computers, networks, troubleshooting, software programs, databases, spreadsheets, and data processing; patience; good research and development skills; a background in finance; and project management skills.

"The best thing about this position is that it has provided a chance for me to explore and educate myself in many new areas and also given me the foundation that should provide an opportunity to become a consultant, in about four or five years. I also like upgrading and training people on the new software, which is part of the job.

"What I like least is the monotony, at times, when projects are not happening. I hate having to look for projects to do. It is also difficult to initiate new projects when there are constant worries about the client's financial situation. This is frustrating because then the company cannot keep current with the new technological advances. But we do our best.

"I would advise others to make sure you get a good education. Be well-rounded in computer knowledge. I'd also suggest that you do an internship while you are still in school."

Meet Tim Lee

Tim Lee, whose work experience includes serving as a network consultant/LAN administrator, started out in a nontechnical field. He earned a bachelor of science degree in economics from Kansas State University in Manhattan, Kansas, and an M.B.A. from Kansas State University in Kansas City, Missouri.

"While working in mutual fund processing, I developed computer system knowledge that led to me taking this job. Before this, I hadn't worked in the field of computers, although they have always interested me," says Lee.

"About half of my day is spent in day-to-day operations management, implementing changes to the system, finding solutions to ongoing problems. I spend about 30 percent of the day on the phone with clients, helping them solve their computer problems. The other 20 percent is spent documenting what I've done that day to help clients.

"To serve in this position, you need to have good problem-solving skills, PC and network experience, experience in customer service/relationship building, organizational skills, networking skills, and the ability to work in a team setting.

"Our company maintains an open-door policy. We tend to work at the client's site, so it's not exactly a casual setting. Our most hectic times are when the computer goes down or when new programs are being implemented. I work an average of forty to fifty hours per week, some evenings.

"What I like best about this job is having the freedom to do what is best for the client. Management really encourages us to be creative with our ideas. We work very much in a team setting, which is nice. My boss is very good at hands-off management style. He trusts me to do what is best for the client. There is a strong entrepreneurial spirit here. I dislike working under the constraints of a state budget, as funds are limited, but on the positive side, it presents challenges in offering the customer the most for the money that is available.

"I'd advise prospective candidates to learn as much as you can about computer software and systems. It's important to develop great problem-solving and customer relationship skills. You have to be a people person. Gain experience as you study. Always keep in mind that your experience will help you in the future."

Meet Brian Killen

Brian Killen earned a bachelor of science degree in computer science from Kansas State University in Manhattan, Kansas. He has enhanced his expertise by attending numerous seminars—anything to do with software engineering development.

"I became interested in computers while in high school," he reveals. "And during college I served in an internship with a computer services organization. I have always wanted to develop products that help people communicate with each other.

"Our work atmosphere is extremely casual. I work in an office where the set hours are Monday through Friday, from 8:30 A.M. until 5:00 P.M. However, the truth is that I usually work fifty to sixty hours per week. During crunch time it can be seventy hours per week. It's a very intense job, definitely not low key.

"Our days are influenced by the projects we are working on at the time," he says, "and the projects run on one- to two-year cycles. In the beginning of a project, there is a lot of thinking, designing, and talking to customers. The latter half of a project is spent sitting at the keyboard and writing code all day. I would say 50 percent of the project is spent writing code. It is the last five months of a project that are the busiest and most stressful.

"The staff convene weekly meetings via teleconference, as some working on the projects are in California and India.

"What I like best is creating the products for people to use. What I like least is the turnaround time for a product. It takes two years to see end results—to feel the full gratification of the job.

"To serve in this position effectively, you need experience in designing user interfaces, software engineering skills, programming skills, networking, protocol development, C++ language, patience, the ability to work in a team setting, the ability to keep the customer in mind, the ability to work well with a diverse group of people, good communication and interpersonal skills, attention to detail, stamina to work on a project for years, persistence, and insight into where the industry is going.

"You really have to like this kind of work to do this job because it's quite demanding. Long, difficult, stressful hours are fairly common. I'd advise others to get as much experience as early as possible because this isn't a job you really come to understand in college. It's a job you learn by doing. Once you experience the doing, you'll be able to determine if this is something that you truly want to make your life's work."

Path 2: Management Analysts and Consultants

"One of the most feared expressions in modern times is 'The computer is down.'"
—Norman Augustine

Help Wanted: Consultant. Selected candidates will plan, analyze, and recommend cost-effective architectures, infrastructures, and standards that adapt to changing business needs, reduce cycle time, and leverage bottom-line results; develop strategy and direction for client/server infrastructure within a large multisite, multiplatform environment; implement new client/server architecture and release phases of client/server initiates. Qualified candidates should possess 3.5+ years of proven experience with large-scale client/server systems, as well as experience with requirements analysis data and process modeling, logical/physical design, and knowledge of structure methodologies and project planning.

Definition of the Career Path

The career called management consulting is a relatively new occupation, born in the 1960s as a result of the growth of the management sciences as a valid academic course of study. Business schools and economics departments across the nation promoted this growth through their literature on the subject of management organization and analysis of work and company efficiency. They began collecting and distributing data on productivity and capacity of organizations, giving companies a greater understanding of the forces affecting them. The 1970s saw the development of small consulting firms with specific areas of expertise, and the 1980s saw the birth of the management consultant generalist who applied general principles of management to individual companies and then offered recommendations.

Management analysts and consultants are problem solvers who piece together puzzles and apply theory to real life in order to suggest solutions to management problems. They are experts at setting up and using computer systems. Companies that wish to reach optimum levels of efficiency and profitability hire management consultants to identify causes and recommend solutions to situations and practices. For example, a rapidly growing small company may need help in designing a better system of control over inventories and expenses, or an established manufacturing company may need assistance in relocating to another state, or a large company may want to reorganize after acquiring a new division. These are just a few of the many organizational problems that management analysts (as they are called in government agencies) and management consultants (as business firms refer to them) help solve.

Consultants' tasks may be sharply defined, such as analyzing the shipping function and streamlining procedures, or broadly defined, such as reorganizing a multinational corporation to take advantage of the synergies that developed when it acquired new businesses.

The work of management analysts and consultants varies by client or employer and from project to project. For example, some projects require a team of consultants, each specializing in one area; at other times, consultants will work independently of each other with the client's managers.

Upon getting an assignment or contract, consultants and analysts try to define the nature and extent of the problem. During this phase of the job, they may analyze data such as annual revenues, employment, or expenditures. Then they interview managers and employees and observe the operations of the organizational unit.

Next, they use their knowledge of management systems and their expertise in a particular area to develop solutions to the problem. In the course of preparing their recommendations, they must take into account the general nature of the business, the relationship the firm has with others in that industry, and the firm's internal organization and culture, as well as information gained through data collection and analysis.

Once they have decided on a course of action, consultants usually report their findings and recommendations to the client, often in writing. In addition, they generally make oral presentations regarding their findings. For some projects, this is all that is required; for others, consultants may assist in the implementation of their suggestions.

Management analysts in government agencies use the same skills as their private-sector colleagues in advising managers in government on many types of issues, most of which are similar to the problems faced by private firms. For example, if an agency is planning to purchase personal computers, it first must determine which type to buy, given its budget and data-processing needs. Management analysts would assess the various types of machines available (by price range) and determine which best meets the department's needs.

Help Wanted: Consultants Who Can Walk on Water. Actually, our standards are slightly lower than that. But if your consulting skills are truly outstanding, then give us a call and tell us about yourself. If you have skills in any of the following areas, we'll walk on water to keep you busy with consulting assignments.

- Informix—4GL
- IEF—Composer
- MS Access, Crystal Reports

If you'd rather be making money than looking for assignments, give us a call. Even if you aren't immediately available—or if you've got miraculous skills not listed—get in touch today!

Possible Job Titles

Computer consultant   Management consultant
Management analyst

Help Wanted: Consultant. Needed for installation, training, and implementing systems. Software applications include associations, small manufacturing, and distribution. Applicants should have good communication skills, as well as PC skills.

Possible Employers

Management consultants may be hired to do whatever helps a client's bottom line. Clients range from companies that are on the cutting edge of their industries and want help in staying ahead to companies that are in trouble and need help staying afloat.

Both public and private organizations use consultants. Some lack the internal resources needed to handle a project; others need a consultant's expertise to determine what resources will be required and what problems may be encountered if they pursue a particular course of action. Still others want to get outside help on how to resolve organizational problems that have already been identified or to avoid troublesome problems that could arise.

Firms providing consulting services range in size from solo practitioners to large international organizations employing thousands of consultants. Some firms specialize by industry, while others specialize by type of business function, such as human resources or information systems. In government, management analysts tend to specialize by type of agency. Consulting services usually are provided on a contractual basis whereby a company solicits proposals from a number of consulting firms specializing in the area in which it needs assistance. These proposals include the estimated cost and scope of the project, staffing requirements, references from a number of previous clients, and the deadline. The company then selects the proposal that best meets its needs.

Many management consulting firms work for federal, state, and local governments. The majority of those working for the federal government are found in the Department of Defense.

Management analysts and consultants are found throughout the country, but employment is concentrated in large metropolitan areas.

Related Occupations

Management analysts and consultants collect, review, and analyze data; make recommendations; and assist in the implementation of their ideas. Other careers that use similar skills are listed.

Computer systems analyst	Investment banker
Economist	Life scientist
Financial analyst	Manager

Operations research analyst	Social scientist
Physical scientist	Sociologist
Researcher	Urban planner

Working Conditions

Management analysts and consultants usually divide their time between their offices and their client's site. Although much of their time is spent indoors in clean, comfortable offices, they may have to visit a client's production facility where conditions may not be so favorable.

Meetings are common and usually serve as forums for brainstorming, discussing new approaches to tackling a problem, and sharing work with other case team members or with the client.

Typically, analysts and consultants work at least forty hours a week, although the figure may certainly vary. Travel, perhaps frequently, may also be required. Overtime is common, especially when project deadlines are near.

Self-employed consultants can set their workloads and hours and work at home. On the other hand, their livelihoods depend on their ability to maintain and expand their client bases. Salaried consultants also must favorably impress potential clients to get and keep clients for their companies.

Computer consultants usually work independently on a contract basis. Some consultants are employed by consulting firms. The hours will vary, as do the lengths of contracts. They may be hourly or monthly or for very extended periods.

Training and Qualifications

No specific academic requirements exist for management analysts and consultants, but nearly all employers require at least a college degree in computer science or a related field, such as business, economics, data processing, statistics, mathematics, or logic.

Educational requirements for entry-level jobs in this field vary widely, but there is an increasing emphasis on scientific and technological applications at the undergraduate level. Employers in private industry generally seek persons with a master's degree in business administration or a related discipline. People hired straight out of school with only a bachelor's degree are generally hired as research associates and will find it difficult to advance up the career ladder unless they return to school for an advanced degree.

Most government agencies hire people with a bachelor's degree and no work experience as entry-level management analysts and often pay for graduate classes in management analysis.

In large consulting firms, beginners are usually assigned research work for consulting teams. (Most major employers run their own programs to train junior consultants in accounting, internal policy, research techniques, and how to work as part of a hard-working team.) The team is responsible for the entire project and each consultant is assigned to a particular area. As consultants gain experience, they may be assigned to work on one specific project full-time, taking on more responsibility and managing their own hours. At the senior level, consultants may supervise entry-level workers and become increasingly involved in seeking out new business. Those with exceptional skills may eventually become partners or principals in the firm. Others with entrepreneurial ambition may open their own firms. At all levels, continuing education is recommended through attending seminars, classes, and conferences.

Many fields of study provide a suitable educational background for this occupation because of the diversity of problem areas addressed by management analysts and consultants. These include most areas of business and management, as well as computer and information sciences and engineering.

Candidates need a background in one or two programming languages and knowledge of a hardware platform (IBM or its clones). Consultants with broader skills know several different programming languages and are familiar with computer-aided software engineering (CASE) technology, and can not only develop new information systems but can integrate new components with old ones. Experts in database management systems, artificial intelligence, technology planning, multilevel database security, and other specific areas are in the stratosphere of consulting.

To be successful, consultants must be exceptional, both analytically and interpersonally. Analytically, they should possess superior problem-solving skills, linear logical thinking, and strong presentation development skills. They also need to be very effective listeners and be able to clearly, concisely, and persuasively communicate their findings to a wide range of people with differing backgrounds and needs.

A high percentage of management consultants are self-employed, partly because business start-up costs are low. Self-employed consultants also can share office space, administrative help, and other resources with other self-employed consultants or small consulting firms, thus reducing overhead costs. Many such firms fail, however, because of an inability to acquire and maintain a profitable client base.

The Institute of Management Consultants (a division of the Council of Consulting Organizations, Inc.) offers the certified management consultant (CMC) designation to those who pass an examination and meet minimum levels of education and experience. Certification is not mandatory for management consultants to practice, but it may give a job seeker a competitive advantage. For more information, contact:

Institute of Management Consultants USA, Inc.
2025 M St. NW, Suite 800
Washington, DC 20036-3309
imcusa.org

Help Wanted: Consultants. We need the best! Our consulting division needs contractors with the following specifications:

- SQL developer
- Microsoft CNE
- Relational DBA
- Java, Active-X

Please state availability and rate.

Earnings

Salaries for management analysts and consultants vary widely by experience, education, and employer. *The Occupational Outlook Handbook*, published by the U.S. Department of Labor, reports that full-time salaried workers have median annual earnings of about $53,400. The middle 50 percent earn between $41,970 and $72,630.

According to the Association of Management Consulting Firms (AMCF), earnings, including bonuses and/or profit sharing for research associates in AMCF member firms, average $39,200; for entry-level consultants, $58,000; for management consultants, $76,300; for senior consultants, $100,300; for junior partners, $135,500; and for senior partners, $259,500.

Typical benefits for salaried analysts and consultants include health and life insurance, a retirement plan, vacation and sick leave, profit sharing, and bonuses for outstanding work. In addition, all travel expenses usually are reimbursed by the employer. Self-employed consultants usually have to maintain their own offices and provide their own benefits.

> **Help Wanted: Consulting Opportunities.** Our Consulting Inc. seeks qualified professionals for local consulting assignments. Outstanding rewards, flexible hours, and long-term engagements await those who wish to advance their career with us. Experience with PeopleSoft software a plus. Fax résumé.

Career Outlook

This is a growing profession, faster than average through 2010, since industry and government will increasingly look to these professions. However, competition for these positions will continue to be intense. Aspiring consultants should prepare for this challenge by achieving strong academic records, gaining work experience that demonstrates competence and maturity, and becoming knowledgeable about accounting and financial issues.

Growth is expected in large consulting firms but also in small consulting firms whose consultants will specialize in specific areas of expertise. Because many small consulting firms fail each year due to lack of managerial expertise and clients, those interested in opening their own firms must have good organizational and marketing skills, plus several years of consulting experience.

Increased competition has forced U.S. industry to take a closer look at its operations. As international and domestic markets become more competitive, firms must use what resources they have more efficiently. Management consultants are being increasingly relied on to help reduce costs, streamline operations, and develop marketing strategies. As businesses downsize and eliminate needed functions, as well as permanent staff, consultants will be used to perform those functions that were previously handled internally. Businesses attempting to expand, particularly into world markets, frequently need the skills of management consultants to help with organizational, administrative, and other issues. Continuing changes in the business environment also are expected to lead to a demand for management consultants. Firms will use consultants to incorporate new technologies, to cope with more numerous and complex government regulations, and to adapt to a changing labor force. As businesses rely more on technology, there are increasing roles for consultants with a technical background, such as engineering or biotechnology, particularly when combined with an M.B.A.

Federal, state, and local agencies also are expected to expand their use of management analysts. In the era of budget deficits, analysts' skills at identifying problems and implementing cost-reduction measures are expected to become increasingly important. However, because almost one-half of the management analysts employed by the federal government work for the Department of Defense, federal employment growth will increase slowly because of cutbacks in the nation's defense budget.

Despite projected rapid employment growth, competition for jobs as management consultants is expected to be keen in the private sector. Because management consultants can come from such diverse educational backgrounds, the pool of applicants from which employers hire is large. Additionally, the independent and challenging nature of the work, combined with high earnings potential, makes this occupation attractive to many. Job opportunities are expected to be best for those with a graduate degree and some industry expertise.

Professional Associations

American Management Association
1601 Broadway
New York, NY 10019
amanet.org

Association of Management Consulting Firms
380 Lexington Ave., Suite 1700
New York, NY 10168
amcf.org

Independent Computer Consultants Association
11131 South Towne Sq., Suite F
St. Louis, MO 63123
icca.org

National Association of Computer Consultant Businesses
1800 Diagonal Rd.
Alexandria, VA 22314
naccb.org

Society for Information Management
401 N. Michigan Ave.
Chicago, IL 60611-4267
simnet.org

U.S. Office of Personnel Management
1900 E St. NW
Washington, DC 20415-0001
opm.gov

Meet Jeffrey Skippen

Jeffrey Skippen earned a bachelor of science degree (with honors) in computer studies/geography from Trent University in Peterborough, Ontario, Canada.

He has attained the status of Novell master CNE and Microsoft certified professional and has served as a senior network management consultant for a government agency.

"I started as a computing services laboratory monitor at Trent University in 1989," he explains. "Then I became a LAN administrator for the Department of Justice, first as a summer student, then as a full-time government employee, and then two additional years as a consultant. For the past two years, I have been acting as the senior network management consultant for a major government department.

"The importance of the computer industry led me to focus on a combined major of geography and computer studies," explains Skippen. "Geography had been my primary interest, but it was becoming obvious to me that computer technology would have a major impact on the future job market. I became a LAN administrator for several summer terms while at school. This eventually led me to choose a career as a network specialist. I always enjoyed tinkering with computers, which were easier for me to understand than other, less defined disciplines, such as geography, English, social sciences, and so on. Computers either worked or they didn't work. They didn't argue with you or make you try to see their point of view. I found the problems presented by computer technology easier to solve than those presented by social and political environments. Best of all, others were amazed when you could fix things that they couldn't possibly understand, no matter how easy it was for you to do so.

"Today my job can be near boring to absolutely terrifying. In my earlier days I was assigned to a project for a cement-mixing company. One of their networked PCs ran an application that mixed the water with the cement, and the company was totally dependent on it. I was doing some work on the computer that ran the mixing application, and something went wrong and the computer would not function properly. Backups and documentation were not concepts this company was familiar with at the time. After about a half hour of downtime, I looked out from the window in the cement silo to see about ten cement trucks lined up waiting to get their loads. All I could think of at the time was that, if I didn't get this system running soon, they would probably be making me a special pair of swimming shoes. Needless to say, I got the system running again and everyone was happy, especially me.

"Every job is a new one with a new combination of variables. The learning process is constant, and you never know what situation you are going to face next. Technology changes daily. You cannot possibly keep up to date with every change. After a while you develop your own methodology of solving problems, and if it is a good, sound methodology, chances are you are going to be successful with it throughout your career. But you must always have a methodology. If you leap before you look, you will eventually get yourself into trouble. If you use a sound methodology to solve problems and you work to perfect it, you will usually come off looking like a hero. And that is the feeling that makes this industry worthwhile—a feeling of self-value and knowing that your contributions made the difference between delight and disaster.

"My hours vary depending on the projects. On the maintenance and installation side of things, you should get used to working weekends and evenings. If you are in day-to-day operations, you will probably work regular hours. Most of us end up doing a combination of these hours and wearing a pocket pager.

"The best part of this job is when I am able to solve complicated problems that made a difference to the client. Many times your efforts will go unnoticed, but eventually you will find the needle in the haystack when someone important is watching.

"Downsides are the times spent in between finding the needle in the haystack. I have to admit I have come close to the borderline of insanity in certain situations. In one situation an entire company was down for several days while I was trying to find out what was wrong with their system. I replaced every piece of hardware, from A to Z, piece by piece—and it still failed. The problem ended up being the client's power supply, but by the time we figured that out I was ready to leave and get into aluminum siding or the clergy.

"A home computer is an essential tool if you are going into this industry. It is your toolbox and your connection to the world—you must have one!

"Computers don't make mistakes—people do! But since people are signing your paychecks, you should be as kind and understanding to them as possible. There is a lot of user frustration out there, and you will always be in the line of fire when you come to fix a problem. Never assume the client has any knowledge, but always talk to the client as though they do."

Meet Tom Teska

Tom Teska earned a bachelor of science degree in computer science from the University of Wisconsin in Madison, Wisconsin.

He has served as a consultant and a certified network engineer. He also received training on Netware 4.x Administration and design and took a class on teaching Novell courses.

"My father opened a ComputerLand store in 1980," says Teska. "When we brought the computers in for his original stock, I started using them. I discovered that I loved working on them and making them do things that no one else could do. From there, I went to helping people use them better. The consulting work lets me do this and work on computers—the best of both worlds.

"Over the years, my job has changed many times. When I worked in the commercial sector, I operated at a very high pace. My work with ComputerLand and Entre stores had me supporting upward of 1,000 companies, with tens of thousands of people. I was typically working sixty to seventy hours a week for months on end.

"I am now employed by a long-term contract consulting firm and the pace is much slower. I report to only one client, supporting fewer than 10,000 people, and now work a standard forty-hour week. When I was assigned to commercial stores, there was no such thing as a typical day. That was actually one of the things I liked about it. I supported people in many different industries, as well as our internal staff. One day I'd be working with bankers, and the next day I'd be helping teachers in an elementary school. Now that I support only one company, I do have typical days. I work in a cubicle with several other support people. We install and support applications and maintain the large WAN that is installed here. I also work on the second-level help desk, which means that I get the problem calls that the first-level people can't solve.

"The thing I like most about being a consultant/support person is being able to get people's PCs to do things that no one else can do. People call me when they've got a problem that they haven't been able to solve and I fix it for them. It makes me feel good to help them like that, and I enjoy the thanks I get from the users in those situations. I also look forward to the actual work with the computers. I have fun while I'm working!

"When I worked in the commercial end of this field, I also got to work with cutting-edge technology. It was really enjoyable to work on new systems that no one had tried before. I find it particularly pleasurable to learn new things.

"My least favorite aspect of this business is having to solve the same problems over and over. That can be frustrating because I know I just solved this problem for someone else three weeks ago but I can't remember exactly how, so I have to do all the same work again. Second, once you've got that memorized and are called on to fix the same problem, you don't learn anything new. Another minor annoyance is that every once in a while I run into a customer who isn't satisfied, no matter what I do. Luckily, this doesn't happen very often. Most of the time, people are very appreciative of my knowledge and efforts.

"I feel that the most important thing about being a consultant is to keep learning. I think it's my job to know more about PCs and networks and software than my customers. Thus, I constantly seek out new information through reading and enrolling in classes in order to be aware of the new strategies and technologies that come to light virtually every day in this ever-changing field."

12

Path 3: Operations Research Analysts

"We live in a time when automation is ushering in a second industrial revolution."
—ADLAI STEVENSON

Help Wanted: Operations Research Analyst. Information Services Group

We are in need of an operations research analyst who will be responsible for understanding, evaluating, and extending the algorithmic components of an Airline Yield Management True Origin and Destination Application.

The successful candidate will have a background in Operations Research with at least two years' experience. A bachelor's degree in operations research is required, with a master's strongly preferred. Experience in airlines or revenue management is desirable but not required. Strong communications skills are required, both written and verbal. The successful candidate will also bring some or all of the following: C/C++ programming experience, object-oriented design experience—Rational-Rose preferred, RDBMS experience—Oracle preferred, UNIX, client server experience—Tuxedo preferred, Windows NT and GUI development skills. We offer a competitive salary and professional opportunity and growth.

Definition of the Career Path

If you're the one in your group who has always been delighted by problem solving via math word problems, operational research analysis might be just the career for you! Acting in the capacity of industry problem solvers, operations research analysts (also called management science analysts) use their computer expertise, along with their scientific, mathematical, and analytical methods, to promote the smooth operations of companies.

Depending on your area of specialization—in industry, government, or international relations—you might be asked to help answer complex questions such as How can a dress manufacturer lay out its patterns to minimize wasted material? How often should the sales force of a frozen yogurt company call on its customers? How many elevators should be installed in a new office building to cut waiting time? What's the most efficient method for routing a long-distance telephone call?

"Operations research" and "management science" are two terms that are used interchangeably to describe the same field (which is also sometimes called decision technology). Basically, operations research is a scientific approach to analyzing problems and making decisions. It uses mathematics and mathematical modeling on computers to forecast the implications of various choices and zero in on the best alternatives.

Developed during World War II, operations research helped take the guesswork out of deploying radar, searching for enemy submarines, getting supplies where they were most needed, and the like. And following the war, numerous peacetime applications emerged.

Manufacturers used operations research to make products more efficiently, schedule equipment maintenance, and control inventory and distribution. Success in these areas led to expansion into strategic and financial planning and into such diverse areas as criminal justice, education, meteorology, and communications.

Operations analysts always begin by learning everything they can about the problem at hand. To accomplish this, they talk with people involved in all aspects of the problem, soliciting their varying perspectives and needs and their input into the solution. They examine available data, separating that which is truly relevant from that which is not. And they focus on practical, workable results, making sure that what they propose is not just a theoretically appealing model but one that will function effectively in the real world.

At this point the operations research analysts present their reports to management, along with recommendations based on their findings. Once there is acceptance of the analyst's work, all parties work together for its implementation.

Operations research analysts use computers extensively in their work. They are typically highly proficient in database management, programming, and in the development and use of sophisticated software programs. Most of the models built by operations research analysts are so complicated that only a computer can solve them efficiently.

The type of problem they usually handle varies by industry. For example, an analyst for an airline would coordinate flight and maintenance scheduling, passenger-level estimates, and fuel consumption to produce a schedule that optimizes all of these factors to ensure safety and produce the most profits. An analyst employed by a hospital would concentrate on a different set of problems—scheduling admissions, managing patient flow, assigning shifts, monitoring use of pharmacy and laboratory services, or forecasting demand for new hospital services.

The role of the operations research analyst varies according to the structure and management philosophy of the firm. Some centralize operations research in one department; others disperse operations research personnel throughout all divisions. Some operations research analysts specialize in one type of application; others are generalists.

Efficiently running a complex organization or operation, such as a large manufacturing plant, an airline, or a military deployment, requires the precise coordination of materials, machines, and people. Operations research analysts help organizations coordinate and operate in the most efficient manner by applying scientific methods and mathematical principles to organizational problems. Managers can then evaluate alternatives and choose the course of action that best meets the organizational goals.

The degree of supervision varies by organizational structure and experience. In some organizations, analysts have a great deal of professional autonomy, while in others, analysts are more closely supervised. Operations research analysts work closely with senior managers, who have a wide variety of support needs. Analysts must adapt their work to reflect these requirements.

Possible Employers

In the United States and around the world, there are a wide variety of job openings in both the public and private sectors. Operations research analysts are employed in most industries. Many large manufacturers, retail chains, and service organizations maintain an in-house staff, ranging in size from one or two operations researchers to a full department. Major employers include computer and data-processing services, commercial banks and savings institutions, insurance carriers, telecommunication companies, engineering and management services firms, manufacturers of transportation equipment, and air carriers. American Airlines, AT&T, Citicorp, Merrill Lynch, American Express, and General Motors are just a few examples of firms that employ sizable numbers of operations research analysts.

The largest employer is the U.S. government—specifically the Departments of Labor, Commerce, Housing and Urban Development, Transportation, Defense, and Health and Human Services, as well as the Government Accounting Office and Congressional Budget Office. All branches of the armed services also work with both civilian and military operations researchers. (In addition, many operations research analysts who work in private industry perform work directly or indirectly related to national defense.) And an increasing number of state and local jurisdictions are hiring both staffers and consultants, as are the governments of other countries.

About two out of ten analysts work for management, research, public relations, and testing agencies that do operations research.

Related Occupations

Operations research analysts apply mathematical principles to large, complicated problems. Workers in other occupations that stress quantitative analysis include computer scientists, engineers, mathematicians, statisticians, and economists. Operations research is closely allied to managerial occupations in that its goal is improved organizational efficiency.

Working Conditions

Operations research analysts generally work regular hours in an office environment. Because they work on projects that are of immediate interest to management, analysts often are under pressure to meet deadlines and often work more than a forty-hour week.

Training and Qualifications

Companies expect that individuals who seek employment have attained at least an undergraduate degree in the computer field or a related area. In fact, employers strongly prefer applicants with at least a master's degree in operations research or management science, or other quantitative disciplines.

More than 150 colleges and universities in the United States and abroad offer degree programs or courses in operations research and closely allied fields.

Employers expect that candidates will have a solid grounding in statistics, probability, calculus, linear algebra, other advanced mathematics, and economics. Because the field relies so heavily on computers, companies will assume you have an understanding of how computers work and how to program them. You will also need a familiarity with up-to-date software, along with an interest in using it as a decision tool. Since research is interdisciplinary, often drawing solutions from engineering, logic, psychology, and other social and political sciences, a well-rounded scientific background proves useful. Exceptional interpersonal and communications skills will serve you well, as will a high degree of initiative, energy, and maturity. You will be expected to perform well on your own or as a member of a team.

Beginning analysts usually do routine work under the supervision of more experienced analysts. As they gain knowledge and experience, they are assigned more complex tasks, with greater autonomy to design models and solve problems. Operations research analysts advance by assuming positions as technical specialists or supervisors. The skills acquired by operations research analysts are useful for higher-level management jobs, and experienced analysts may leave the field altogether to assume nontechnical managerial or administrative positions.

Employers often sponsor skill-improvement training for experienced workers, helping them keep up with new developments in operations research techniques, as well as advances in computer science. Some analysts attend advanced university classes on these subjects at their employer's expense.

Earnings

According to the U.S. Department of Labor, median annual salaries for operations research analysts are about $53,400. The middle 50 percent earn between $40,500 and $70,800 a year.

Median annual earnings in selected areas are as follows:

Computer and data-processing services	$65,420
Federal government	$62,990
Aircraft and parts	$52,960
Engineering and architectural services	$47,480

Career Outlook

Organizations are increasingly using operations research and management science techniques to improve productivity and quality and to reduce costs. This reflects growing acceptance of a systematic approach to decision making by top managers. This trend is expected to continue and should greatly stimulate demand for these workers in the years ahead.

Those seeking employment as operations research or management science analysts who hold a master's or Ph.D. degree should find good opportunities through the year 2010. The number of openings generated each year as a result of employment growth and the need to replace those leaving the occupation is expected to exceed the number of persons graduating with master's and Ph.D. degrees from management science or operations research programs.

Graduates with only a bachelor's degree in operations research or management science should find opportunities as research assistants or analyst assistants in a variety of related fields that allow them to use their quantitative abilities. Only the most highly qualified are likely to find employment as operations research or management science analysts.

Employment of operations research analysts is expected to grow much faster than the average for all occupations due to the increasing importance of quantitative analysis in decision making. Much of the job growth is expected to occur in the transportation, manufacturing, finance, and service sectors, areas where the use of quantitative analysis can achieve dramatic improvements in operating efficiency and profitability. More airlines, for example, are using operations research to determine the best flight and maintenance schedules, select the best routes to service, analyze customer characteristics, and control fuel consumption, among other things. Motel chains are beginning to use operations research to improve their efficiency by analyzing automobile traffic patterns and customer attitudes to determine location, size, and style of proposed new motels. Like other management support functions, operations research grows by its own success. When one firm in an industry increases productivity by adopting a new procedure, its competitors usually follow. This competitive pressure will contribute to demand for operations research analysts.

Demand also should be strong in the manufacturing sector as firms expand existing operations research staffs in the face of growing domestic and foreign competition. More manufacturers are using mathematical models to study the operations of the organization. For example, analysts will be needed to determine the best way to control product inventory, distribute finished products, and decide where sales offices should be based. In addition, increasing factory automation will require more operations research analysts to alter existing models or develop new ones for production layout, robotics installation, work schedules, and inventory control.

Professional Associations

Canadian Operational Research Society
P.O. Box 2225, Station D
Ottawa, ON K1P 5W4
Canada
cors.ca

Institute for Operations Research and the Management Sciences
901 Elkridge Landing Rd., Suite 400
Linthicum, MD 21090-2909
informs.org

Military Operations Research Society
1703 N. Beauregard St., Suite 450
Alexandria, VA 22311-1717
mors.org

13

Path 4: Computer Operators and Programmers

"If it keeps up, man will atrophy all his limbs but the push-button finger."
—Frank Lloyd Wright

Help Wanted: Computer Operator, 2nd Shift. Our manufacturing company has an opening for a 2nd-shift computer operator. We are a leading designer and manufacturer of electrical equipment, components, and controls that provide for the economical, safe, and reliable delivery of high-quality electrical power.

A high school diploma and 2+ years' experience as a computer operator are required. We also seek a background in IBM Mainframe—VSE/SP—and knowledge of VTAM commands. Familiarity with XBMS software is a plus but not required.

Send résumé in confidence.

Definition of the Career Path

Computer and peripheral equipment operators oversee the operation of computer hardware systems, ensuring that these machines are used as efficiently as possible. This means that operators must be proactive—anticipate problems before they occur and take preventive action, as well as solve problems that do occur.

Duties of computer and peripheral equipment operators vary with the policies of the employer, the size of the installation, and the kind of equipment used. Working from operating instructions prepared by programmers, users, or operations managers, computer operators set controls on the computer and on peripheral devices required to run a particular job. Computer operators or, in some large installations, peripheral equipment operators load the equipment with tapes, disks, and paper as needed. While the computer is running (which may be twenty-four hours a day for large computers), computer operators monitor the computer console and respond to operating and computer messages. Messages indicate the individual specifications of each job being run. If an error message occurs, operators must locate and solve the problem or terminate the program.

Traditionally, peripheral equipment operators have to prepare printouts and other output for distribution to computer users. Operators also maintain log books listing each job that is run and events such as machine malfunctions that occurred during their shift. In addition, computer operators may supervise and train peripheral equipment operators and computer operator trainees. They also may help programmers and systems analysts test and debug new programs.

As the trend toward networking computers accelerates, a growing number of these workers are operating PCs and minicomputers. More and more, establishments are recognizing the need to connect all their computers to enhance productivity. In many offices, factories, and other work settings, PCs and minicomputers serve as the center of such networks, often referred to as local area networks (LANs) or multi-user systems. Although some of these computers are operated by users in the area, many require the services of full-time operators. The tasks performed are very similar to those performed on the larger computers.

As organizations continue to use computers in more areas of operation, they are also fulfilling opportunities to increase the productivity of computer operations. Automation, which traditionally has been the application of computer technology to other functional areas of an organization, is now reaching the computer room. Sophisticated software, coupled with robotics, now exists, enabling the computer to perform many routine tasks formerly done by computer and peripheral equipment operators. Scheduling, loading and downloading programs, mounting tapes, rerouting messages, and running periodic reports can be done without the intervention of an operator. These improvements will change what computer operators do in the future. However, in the computer centers that lack this level of automation, some computer operators still may be responsible for tasks traditionally done by peripheral equipment operators. As technology advances, many computer operators will essentially monitor an automated system. As the role of operators changes due to new technology, their responsibilities may shift to system security, troubleshooting, desk help, network problems, and maintaining large databases.

Computer/console operators operate and monitor computer runs. They follow the programmers' instructions for processing the data that goes into the computer. They make sure that the computer has been loaded with the correct magnetic tape or disks and watch closely for error lights that indicate that the computer is not operating properly.

Help Wanted: Programmers. Our successful consulting firm is expanding into the computer consulting market. Highest hourly rates paid for experienced developers. Benefits include major medical, life, dental, and vision. Join a growing company. If you have been on your job for three to five years and believe you are underpaid, you need to contact us. Send résumé.

Computer programmers write and maintain the detailed instructions, called programs or software, that list, in a logical order, the steps that computers must execute to perform their functions. In many large organizations, programmers follow descriptions prepared by systems analysts who have carefully studied the task that the computer system is going to perform. These descriptions list the input required, the steps the computer must follow to process data, and the desired arrangement of the output. Some organizations, particularly smaller ones, do not employ systems analysts. Instead, workers called programmer-analysts are responsible for both systems analysis and programming.

Regardless of setting, programmers write specific programs by breaking down each step into a logical series of instructions the computer can follow. They then code these instructions in a conventional programming language or one of the more advanced artificial intelligence or object-oriented languages.

The transition from a mainframe environment to primarily a PC-based environment has blurred the once rigid distinction between the programmer and the user. Increasingly, adept users are taking over many of the tasks previously performed by programmers. For example, the growing use of packaged software, such as spreadsheet and database management software packages, allows users to write simple programs to access data and perform calculations.

Programmers in software development companies may work directly with experts from various fields to create software, either programs designed for specific clients or packaged software for general use, ranging from games and educational software to programs for desktop publishing, financial planning, and spreadsheets. Much of the programming being done today is in the area of packaged software development, one of the most rapidly growing segments of the computer industry.

Despite the prevalence of packaged software, many programmers are involved in updating, debugging, and modifying code for existing programs. When making changes to a section of code, called a routine, programmers need to make other users aware of the task that the routine is to perform. They do this by inserting comments in the coded instructions so that others can understand the program. Programmers using computer-aided software engineering (CASE) tools can concentrate on writing the unique parts of the program because the tools automate various pieces of the program being built. This also yields more reliable and consistent programs and increases programmers' productivity by eliminating some of the routine steps.

When a program is ready to be tested, programmers give it a test run to ensure that the instructions are correct and will produce the desired information. They prepare sample data that test every part of the program and, after trial runs, review the results to see if any errors were made. If errors do occur, the programmer must make the appropriate modifications and recheck the program until it produces the desired results. This is what is known as debugging the program.

Finally, programmers working in a mainframe environment prepare instructions for the computer operator, who will run the program.

Programs vary depending on the type of information to be accessed or generated. For example, the instructions involved in updating financial records are different from those required to duplicate conditions onboard an aircraft for pilots training in a flight simulator. Although simple programs can be written in a few hours, programs that use complex mathematical formulas or many data files may require more than a year of work. In most cases, several programmers may work together as a team under a senior programmer's supervision.

Programmers often are grouped into two broad types: applications programmers and systems programmers. Applications programmers usually are oriented toward business, engineering, or science. They write software designed to handle specific jobs, such as a program used in an inventory control system or one to guide a missile after it has been fired. They also may work alone to revise existing packaged software. Systems programmers, on the other hand, maintain the software that controls the operation of an entire computer system. These workers make changes in the sets of instructions that determine how the central processing unit of the system handles the various jobs it has been given and communicates with peripheral equipment, such as terminals, printers, and disk drives. Because of their knowledge of the entire computer system, systems programmers often help applications programmers determine the source of problems that may occur with their programs.

Possible Employers

Computer operators and peripheral equipment operators hold about 250,000 jobs. Although jobs for computer and peripheral equipment operators are found in almost every industry, most are in data-processing service firms, wholesale trade establishments, manufacturing companies, financial institutions, and government agencies. These organizations have data-processing needs that require large computer installations. A growing number are employed by firms in the computer and data-processing services industry, as more companies contract out the operation of their data-processing centers.

More than one out of ten computer and peripheral equipment operators work part-time.

Computer programmers hold about 650,000 jobs. They are employed in most industries, with the largest concentrations in computer and office equipment manufacturing, data-processing service organization firms that write and sell software, companies that provide engineering and management services, financial institutions, insurance carriers, and government agencies. Applications programmers work for all types of firms, whereas systems programmers usually work for organizations with large computer centers or for firms that manufacture computers or develop software.

A growing number of programmers are employed on a temporary or contract basis. Rather than hiring programmers as permanent employees and then laying them off after a job is completed, employers increasingly are contracting with temporary help agencies, consulting firms, or directly with programmers themselves. A marketing firm, for example, may only require the services of several programmers to write and debug the software necessary to get a new database management system running. Such jobs may last for several months to a year or longer.

Help Wanted: Programmer. We are a national provider of practice management software to the medical community.

We are currently seeking an experienced database programmer to work in the UNIX environment writing custom programs, conversions, and interfaces to our software. Qualified applicants will possess a B.S.C.S. and three to five years' database programming experience. Medical Manager/Data Merge experience a definite plus.

We offer excellent working conditions and competitive compensation. Please fax résumé.

Related Occupations

Other occupations involving interaction with computers include computer scientists, systems analysts, and computer service technicians. Other jobs in which workers operate electronic office equipment include data entry keyers, secretaries, typists and word processors, and typesetters and compositors.

Programmers must pay great attention to detail as they write and debug programs. Other professional workers who must be detail oriented include statisticians, engineers, financial analysts, accountants, auditors, actuaries, and operations research analysts.

Help Wanted: Computer Operator—Full-Time. Bank is seeking an experienced computer operator. Requirements are a strong knowledge of IBM or equivalent computer systems, ability to meet deadlines. Excellent attendance and punctuality and willingness to engage in professional development activities. If you meet these qualifications, please send résumé, including salary history.

Working Conditions

Computer operators usually work about thirty-five to forty hours per week in well-lighted, well-ventilated, comfortable rooms. Because many organizations use their computers twenty-four hours a day, seven days a week, computer and peripheral equipment operators may be required to work evening or night shifts and weekends. Shift assignments generally are made on the basis of seniority. Automated operations will lessen the need for shift work because many companies let the computer take over all operations during less desirable working hours.

Because computer operators spend a lot of time in front of a computer monitor, as well as performing repetitive tasks such as loading and unloading printers, they may be susceptible to eyestrain, back discomfort, and hand and wrist problems.

Computer programmers usually work in offices that are clean and comfortable. Working hours usually number thirty-five to forty hours per week but not necessarily nine o'clock to five o'clock. Regular schedules may include evening or weekend hours. In addition, programmers may work longer hours or on weekends to meet deadlines or fix critical problems that occur during off hours.

Because programmers also spend long periods in front of a computer monitor typing at a keyboard, they too are susceptible to eyestrain, back discomfort, and hand and wrist problems.

Help Wanted: Computer Programmer. International company seeking professional with knowledge of Visual Basic, FoxPro, and Novell network. The chosen candidate will streamline computer department operations. Good salary and benefits for the right person. Call to arrange interview.

Training and Qualifications

Previous work experience is the key to landing an operator job in many large establishments. Employers look for specific, hands-on experience in the type of equipment and related operating systems that they use. Additionally, computer-related formal training, perhaps through a junior college or technical school, is recommended. As computer technology changes and data-processing centers become more automated, more employers will require candidates for the remaining operator jobs to have formal training, as well as experience.

Workers usually receive on-the-job training to become acquainted with their employer's equipment and routines. The length of training varies with the job and the experience of the worker. Training is also offered by the armed forces and by some computer manufacturers.

Because computer technology changes so rapidly, operators must be adaptable and willing to learn. Greater analytical and technical expertise are also needed to deal with the unique or higher-level problems that the computer is not programmed to handle, particularly by operators who work in automated data centers.

Computer and peripheral equipment operators must be able to communicate well to work effectively with programmers or users, as well as with other operators. Computer operators also must be able to work independently because they may have little or no supervision.

Peripheral equipment operators may advance to computer operator jobs. A few computer operators may advance to supervisory jobs. Through on-the-job experience and additional formal education, some computer and peripheral equipment operators may advance to jobs as programmers or analysts, although the move into these jobs is becoming more difficult as employers increasingly require candidates for more skilled computer professional jobs to possess at least a bachelor's degree. Others may become specialists in areas such as network operations or support.

There are no universal training requirements for programmers because employers' needs are so varied. Computer applications have become so widespread that computer programming is taught at most public and private vocational schools, community and junior colleges, and universities. However, the level of education and quality of training that employers seek have been rising due to the growth in the number of qualified applicants and the increasing complexity of some programming tasks. Although some programmers obtain two-year degrees or certificates, bachelor's degrees are now commonly required. Candidates usually have earned a bachelor of arts or bachelor of science degree, often in computer science or information systems. Graduate degrees are required for some jobs. Employers who use computers for business applications prefer to hire people who have had college courses in management information systems (MIS) and business, and who possess strong programming skills. Knowledge of a variety of programming languages is highly desirable. General business skills and experience related to the operations of the firm are preferred by employers as well.

Most systems programmers hold a four-year degree in computer science. Extensive knowledge of a variety of operating systems is essential. This includes being able to configure the operating system to work with different types of hardware and adapting the operating system to best meet the needs of the particular organization. They also must be able to work with leading database systems.

The Institute for Certification of Computing Professionals confers the designation certified computing professional (CCP) to those who have at least four years of experience or two years of experience and a college degree. To qualify, persons must pass a core examination, plus exams in two specialty areas, or an exam in one specialty area and two computing languages. Those with little or no experience may be tested for certification as an associate computer professional (ACP). Certification is not mandatory, but it may give a job seeker a competitive advantage.

When hiring programmers, employers look for people with the necessary programming skills who can think logically and pay close attention to detail. The job calls for patience, persistence, and the ability to do exacting analytical work, especially under pressure. Ingenuity and imagination are also particularly important when programmers design solutions and test their work for potential failures. Increasingly, interpersonal skills are important, as programmers are expected to work in teams and interact directly with users. The ability to work with abstract concepts and do technical analysis is especially important for systems programmers because they work with the software that controls the computer's operation.

Beginning programmers may spend their first weeks on the job attending training classes since each business has its own development methodology, processes, and tools. After this initial instruction, they may work alone on simple assignments or on a team with more experienced programmers. Either way, they generally must spend at least several months working under close supervision. Because of rapidly changing technology, programmers must continuously update their training by taking courses sponsored by their employer or software vendors.

For skilled workers, the prospects for advancement are good. In large organizations, they may be promoted to lead programmer and be given supervisory responsibilities. Some applications programmers may move into systems programming after they gain experience and take courses in systems software. With general business experience, both applications programmers and sys-

---

Help Wanted: Programmer. We are a leader in the education industry and have been for more than 120 years. We are seeking an experienced programmer for our local facility. You'll be responsible for developing, testing, maintaining, and troubleshooting a variety of platforms, including ES9000 and RS6000. Ideal candidate will have the ability to work well on a team and independently. Position requires a bachelor's degree in computer science or a related field, experience, one to two years of COBOL programming experience, and good communication skills. Programming in natural and design skills desirable. Will consider a new graduate. Our working environment is business casual, and we provide many excellent benefits, including 401(k), profit sharing, and medical/ dental insurance. Please forward résumé.

tems programmers may become systems analysts or be promoted to a managerial position. Other programmers, with specialized knowledge and experience with a language or operating system, may work in research and development areas such as multimedia or Internet technology. As employers increasingly contract out programming jobs, more opportunities should arise for experienced programmers with expertise in a specific area to work as consultants.

Earnings

Recent studies indicate that full-time computer operators have a median income of about $27,600 a year. The middle 50 percent earn between $21,200 and $35,300. The lowest 10 percent earn less than $17,350, and the top 10 percent earn more than $43,900.

According to Robert Half International Inc., the average starting salaries for computer operators range from $28,250 to $40,500. Salaries generally are higher in large organizations than in small ones.

In the federal government, the average annual salary for all computer operators is about $37,500.

Median earnings of programmers who work full-time is about $57,500 a year. The middle 50 percent earn between about $44,850 and $74,500 a year. The lowest 10 percent earn less than $25,020, and the highest 10 percent, more than $93,000.

According to Robert Half International Inc., starting salaries range from $58,500 to $90,000 for applications development programmers/developers and $54,000 to $77,500 for software development programmers/analysts. Starting salaries for Internet programmers/analysts range from $56,500 to $84,000.

Salaries and benefits for computer programmers are generally higher than those earned by nonsupervisory workers in other fields. Most companies offer paid vacations and holidays, along with sick leave and medical insurance. Other benefits offered might be pension plans, profit sharing, and tuition reimbursement.

Programmers working in the West and Northeast earn somewhat more than those working in the South and Midwest. On average, systems programmers earn more than applications programmers.

According to the National Association of Colleges and Employers, graduates with a bachelor's degree in computer programming earn average starting salaries of about $48,600.

Career Outlook

Employment of computer and peripheral equipment operators is expected to decline sharply through the year 2010. Many experienced operators are expected to compete for the small number of openings that will arise each year to replace workers who transfer to other occupations or leave the labor force.

Advances in technology have reduced both the size and the cost of computer equipment while increasing the capacity for data storage and processing. These improvements in technology have fueled an expansion in the use of computers in such areas as factory and office automation, telecommunications, medicine, and education.

The expanding use of software that automates computer operations gives companies the option of making systems user-friendly, greatly reducing the need for operators. Even if firms continue to employ operators in some capacity—which, for many, is extremely likely in the near future—these new technologies will require operators to monitor a greater number of operations at the same time and be capable of solving a broader range of problems that may arise. The result is that fewer and fewer operators will be needed to perform more highly skilled work.

Computer operators or peripheral equipment operators who are displaced by automation may be reassigned to support staffs that maintain PC networks or assist other members of the organization. Operators who keep up with changing technology, by updating their skills and enhancing their training, should have the best prospects of moving into other areas such as network administration. Others may be retrained to perform different job duties, such as supervising an entire operations center, maintaining automation packages, or analyzing computer operations to recommend ways to increase productivity. In the future, operators who wish to continue in the computer field will need to know more about programming, automation software, graphics interfaces, and open systems to take advantage of changing opportunities.

Employment of programmers is expected to grow about as fast as the average for all occupations through the year 2010. Employment is not expected to grow as rapidly as in the past as improved software and programming techniques continue to simplify programming tasks. In addition, greater use of packaged software—such as word-processing and spreadsheet packages—should continue to moderate the growth in demand for applications programmers. As the level of technological innovation and sophistication increases, users will be able to design, write, and implement more of their own programs to meet their changing needs.

Although the proportion of programmers leaving the occupation each year is smaller than that of most occupations, most of the job openings for programmers will result from replacement needs. The majority of programmers who leave, transfer to other occupations, such as manager or systems analyst. Jobs for both systems and applications programmers, however, should remain particularly plentiful in data-processing service firms, software houses, and computer consulting businesses. These types of establishments remain part of the fastest-growing industries in computer and data-processing services. As companies look to control costs, those in need of programming services should look to this industry to meet these needs.

As computer usage expands, however, the demand for skilled programmers will increase as organizations seek new applications for computers and improvements to the software already in use. Employers are increasingly interested in programmers who can combine areas of technical expertise or who are adaptable and able to learn and incorporate new skills. One area of progress will be data communications. Networking computers so that they can communicate with each other is necessary to achieve the greater efficiency that organizations require to remain competitive. Object-oriented languages will increasingly be used in the years ahead, further enhancing the productivity of programmers. Programmers will be creating and maintaining expert systems and embedding these technologies in more and more products.

Strategy for Finding the Jobs

The number and quality of applicants for programmer jobs have increased, so employers have become more selective. Graduates of two-year programs in data processing and people with less than a two-year degree or its equivalent in work experience are facing especially strong competition for programming jobs. Competition for entry-level positions even affects applicants with a bachelor's degree. Many observers expect opportunities for people without college degrees to diminish in coming years as programming tasks become more complex and more sophisticated skills and experience are demanded by employers. Prospects should be good for college graduates with knowledge of a variety of programming languages, particularly C++ and other object-oriented languages, as well as newer languages that apply to computer networking, database management, and artificial intelligence. To remain competitive, college graduates should keep up to date with the latest skills and technologies.

Many employers prefer to hire applicants with previous experience in the field. Firms also desire programmers who develop a technical specialization in areas such as client/server programming, multimedia technology, graphic user interface, or fourth- and fifth-generation programming tools. Therefore, people who want to become programmers can enhance their chances by combining work experience with the appropriate formal training. Students should try to gain experience by participating in a college work-study program or undertaking an internship. Students also can greatly improve their employment prospects by taking courses such as accounting, management, engineering, or science-allied fields in which applications programmers are in demand. With the expansion of client/server environments, employers will continue to look for programmers with strong technical skills, as well as good interpersonal and business skills.

Professional Associations

Association for Computing Machinery
One Astor Plaza
1515 Broadway
New York, NY 10036-5701
acm.org

Institute for Certification of Computing Professionals
2350 E. Devon Ave., Suite 115
Des Plaines, IL 60018-4610
iccp.org

Network and Systems Professionals Association, Inc.
7044 S. Thirteenth St.
Oak Creek, WI 53154
naspa.com

Meet Kathy Hargreaves

Kathy Hargreaves earned a bachelor of arts degree from the University of California, Los Angeles (UCLA); an M.F.A. from UCLA (both in painting/sculpture/graphic arts); and an M.A. in computer science from the University of Massachusetts in Boston. She has worked as a self-employed software consultant since 1989.

"I was turned to computers by a very enthusiastic boss from my first real job after college," she says. "We were both art graduates, so the technical world was very esoteric. Of course, I was completely terrified of the whole technical thing. Later, I began working as a typesetter in a big firm in San Francisco. The individual who was setting up and programming the computer system waltzed in at 11:00 A.M., while we had to punch time clocks! The work was already close to what I later found out was writing macros, and I'd already been taking programming courses, so I found out about a reentry program for women and minorities at a local university and decided to go for it.

"Now, I work at home mostly," she says. "If I'm working hourly, it's harder to not go overboard with the hours than you might think. I try to restrict programming to the morning. Basically, I get up, eat breakfast, and go upstairs to the computer until it's time to exercise.

"Work ranges from simple typing to writing macros in typesetting language. I try to stay relaxed about it. Basically, I avoid strict deadline jobs so that I can control the hours that I work. In total, I work about twenty to thirty hours per week.

"I enjoy working out of my house and make good use of the phone and E-mail to keep in touch with my clients," she says.

"I really like not having to deal with a boss face-to-face or go into an office (often without windows that open) for set times of the day. I enjoy the fact that I don't have to deal with the hassle of commuting to work. On the other hand, I least like having to find work and clients who don't answer E-mail or make it clear what they want and for how much. Or those who don't even know what they want.

"I'd advise others who are considering this type of work to avoid this occupation unless you really love doing it."

14

Path 5: Computer Sales and Service

"A computer will do what you tell it to do, but that may be different from what you had in mind."
—JOSEPH WEISENBAUM, QUOTED IN *TIME*

Help Wanted: Computer Network Sales Consultant. Are you someone who enjoys assessing business needs and providing solutions?

We require:
- Strong technical knowledge
- College degree
- 1–3 years' experience

Send résumé immediately!

Definition of the Career Path

Success in a sales career (in any field) requires knowledge of the product or service being offered, in addition to expertise in the art of selling. Thus, persons interested in a career in computer sales need to learn everything possible about computers and how they operate, in addition to gaining sufficient knowledge and understanding of the psychology of sales.

All salespeople must be able to convince prospective customers of the value of their products and services. This involves demonstrating the equipment and pointing out its design and engineering superiority and the various advantages it provides the consumer over competitive products in the marketplace. To accomplish this, sales professionals need to possess a thorough familiarity with electronics and a firm grasp of the particulars involved in the line of computers and the kinds of software on the market. These are the products that will enable the user to accomplish such tasks as billing, word processing, accounting, and so on.

There is a fundamental difference between computer salespeople who work in a store and those who are involved in outside sales. In the first case, customers already have some interest and have been drawn into a store either because of word of mouth; special promotions; or ads the company may have placed in newspapers, on radio, or on TV.

This is not to intimate, however, that retail sales clerks must not actively make use of selling expertise, because they certainly do. Interested parties still must be converted to customers. In some cases, salespeople may succeed in upgrading a prospective customer from an inexpensive, beginning-level personal computer to one that can do more sophisticated applications in a fraction of the time. They can also be instrumental in selling customers peripheral and add-on equipment that they will need for their computers—more sophisticated or color video display terminals, for instance; modems for telephone transmission of computer messages; surge protectors to guard against power surges; cables; and, of course, software, depending on what the customer wants to do with the computer.

Outside salespeople, on the other hand, must usually work primarily on their own, developing their own lists of prospects, working from leads supplied by the company via mail, fax, E-mail, or phone. In addition to this, these sales professionals must be able to develop lists of prospective clients to call on through the use of phone books and business directories, chamber of commerce directories, and other reference materials. Further, they may seek leads from their business associates, personal connections, satisfied customers, trade publications, and anywhere else they can think of.

Whatever the source of the lead, the sales professional may have to visit the client's office to demonstrate the computer system to all involved, including the person who may be using the computer, the department supervisor, the person who must approve the purchase, and any other interested persons. Often the salesperson may have to make one or more return trips to make a sale.

Computer repairers install equipment, do preventive maintenance, and correct problems. They work on computers (mainframes, minis, and micros), peripheral equipment, and word-processing systems. Some repairers service both computers and office equipment. They may make cable and wiring connections when installing equipment and work closely with electricians, who install the wiring.

Even with preventive maintenance, computers and other machines do break down. Repairers run diagnostic programs to locate malfunctions. Although some of the most modern and sophisticated computers have a self-diagnosing capacity that identifies problems, computer repairers must know enough about systems software to determine if the malfunction is in the hardware or in the software.

Help Wanted: Computer Service Rep. Progressive computer rental services company is seeking a customer-service oriented driver to deliver and install computer equipment. Knowledge of current hardware and peripherals required, along with a degree in computer science or a related field. A clean driving record and valid driver's license also required. Send résumé.

Possible Job Titles

Account executive	Computer service person
Computer account representative	Computer technician
Computer salesperson	Retail store manager

Possible Employers

Jobs in computer sales fall into two categories: (1) employment by vendors or manufacturers and (2) jobs in retail stores. Vendors sell directly to the industry. They try to meet the needs of computer users such as banks, insurance companies, colleges and universities and school systems, accounting and business agencies, hospitals and health-care facilities, government agencies, and others in all sectors of the economy. Sales personnel may work out of the vendor's headquarters or be assigned to district sales offices throughout the country.

With the proliferation of PCs in the home and industry, computers are now sold in thousands of retail establishments located all over the country. These include computer stores; office equipment stores; department stores;

furniture and appliance dealers, as well as independent sales organizations that sell directly to industry, including value-added resellers, system integrators, and others who serve as consultants and agents in matching computer systems to the needs of commercial and industrial firms.

Some of the large computer stores also have outside sales forces who call on schools, industrial firms, and government agencies, as well as catalog or mail-order divisions that take orders over the phone from customers who have received the company's catalog.

Computer, automated teller, and office machine repairers hold about 172,000 jobs. Some work mainly on computer equipment, while others specialize in repairing office machines or automated teller machines. About half are employed by wholesalers of computers and other office equipment, including the wholesaling divisions of equipment manufacturers, and by firms that provide maintenance services for a fee. Others work for retail establishments and some with organizations that service their own equipment. About one in seven is self-employed.

Repairers work throughout the country, even in relatively small communities. Most repairers, however, work in large cities, where computer and office equipment is concentrated.

Related Occupations

Persons involved in selling computers can transfer their expertise to sell almost any product or service, particularly those in the area of technology. Sales professionals perform similar tasks to travel agents, real estate agents, insurance agents, financial representatives, and advertising account executives. Those involved in service can also transfer their skills to servicing any other type of product, particularly one involving electronics or technology.

Help Wanted: Computer Marketing Rep. Seeking an enthusiastic professional field sales rep with strong technology background. Retail channel experience a plus. Degree in marketing, sales, or computer science desired. Must have exceptional presentation skills, be capable of managing a territory, and be able to clearly communicate technical information. Responsibilities will include sales, training, and account management for cutting-edge PC products from one of the world's largest technology companies.

Working Conditions

Those involved in computer sales, particularly retail sales, may work peak hours, including evenings and weekends. Usually a forty-hour week is assigned, except during special sales or promotions, when additional hours may be expected.

Computer service personnel usually work forty hours per week in a variety of offices, some of which they may have to travel to. In emergency situations, overtime may be necessary. Shift work is not uncommon. Some are on call twenty-four hours.

Training and Qualifications

Although you do not necessarily have to have a college degree to get a job in retail sales, it will be a definite plus not only in securing the job and performing it well but in advancing to higher and better-paying jobs. The core curriculum for college or university centers on courses in computer science. Besides this concentration, you should take required and elective courses in math (differential and integral calculus, analytical geometry, and applied modern algebra), natural sciences (physics is especially important), the humanities (literature, art, and history), and the social sciences. Also important are business courses such as marketing and sales. A knowledge of speech communication or public speaking can help you in making presentations before small and large groups. More than 75 percent of those currently involved in computer sales, both in the retail and corporate levels, are college graduates.

Look into the availability of PC users' clubs. By joining and participating in such groups, you can become more familiar with computer terminology and procedures, which will help you when you begin to look for employment in the industry.

Success in sales is based largely on how well you understand people—what motivates them and why they buy. Thus, exposure to the public can be invaluable in learning how to deal successfully with people. You must be ambitious, aggressive, independent, organized, detail-minded, an able listener, and a good communicator. If you are truly computer savvy, you will be able to ascertain the customers' needs and provide a viable solution.

Because of the need to keep abreast of all of the most recent developments in the field, a sales representative may periodically be expected to attend seminars on the use of the product and on software systems or applications as they are developed. Such seminars may be offered by the employers or vendor, or by the manufacturers, in the case of business-to-business sales. Such sales training programs can range from a few days, in the case of a retail store, to several months of intensive training, in the case of a large vendor. These sessions are supplemented by small sales meetings of a day or two, stressing new products and applications, in the case of the retail store, and new features of the product or computer system, in the case of the vendor.

In addition to this, retail sales employees, and to a certain extent vendor sales reps, are expected to know how to handle the paperwork involved in making out sales records, receiving cash, handling charge slips and coupons, and so on. Sales personnel may also be expected to handle returns and exchanges, help stock shelves, make price tags, put up displays, and help take inventory. But the bottom line is doing whatever is necessary to satisfy the customer or client.

To perform service on computers, employers will seek candidates with a minimum of a high school education, plus training in electronics and course work in mathematics, science, and electronics. Many companies prefer several years of electronics at a technical school or college and/or practical experience.

Personal attributes include good vision (with no color blindness) and the ability to work long hours and to deal with stress. Desirable qualities also include the ability to deal well with customers, to explain details, and to work with little supervision. Candidates should be mechanically skillful, interested in electronics, and able to complete precise work with manual dexterity.

Earnings

Earnings vary widely for sales personnel, depending on performance. Experienced sales reps can earn more than $100,000 a year, more than their management superiors. The median income of sales reps (often based on a combination of straight salary and commission) is about $35,000 to $505,000 per year. Outside salespeople earn median salaries of $55,000 to $70,000 per year. Median salaries for inside sales personnel is about $40,000. Benefits are also important—some companies offer paid vacations, health insurance, retirement plans, bonuses, extra vacation time, trips, and prizes for bettering company quotas.

The *Occupational Outlook Handbook*, published by the U.S. Department of Labor, reports that average salaries for service technicians are about $600 per week. The middle 50 percent fall between $472 and $768; the bottom 10 percent, less than $380; and the top 10 percent, more than $936.

Career Outlook

With the popularity of computers continuing to increase at a steady rate, opportunities are excellent for persons interested in embarking on careers in computer sales. For those with at least a bachelor's degree, experience in sales (of any kind), and knowledge of computers and the computer world, the chances of employment are especially good. Larger cities provide increased opportunities.

Employment of computer and office machine repairers is expected to grow faster than the average for all occupations through the year 2010. Demand for computer repairers will increase as the amount of computer equipment increases. Organizations throughout the economy should continue to automate in search of greater productivity and improved service. The development of new computer applications and lower computer prices will also spur demand. More repairers will be needed to install, maintain, and repair these machines.

Computer and office machine repairers work throughout the country, even in relatively small communities.

Professional Associations

Association for Computing Machinery
One Astor Plaza
1515 Broadway
New York, NY 10036-5701
acm.org

Communications Workers of America
501 Third St. NW
Washington, DC 20001-2797
cwa-union.org

CompTIA (Computing Technology Industry Association)
1815 S. Meyers Rd., Suite 300
Oakbrook Terrace, IL 60181-5228
comptia.org

Computer & Communications Industry Association
666 Eleventh St. NW
Washington, DC 20001
ccianet.org

Electronics Technicians Association
502 N. Jackson
Greencastle, IN 46135
eta-sda.com

United States Telecom Association
1401 H St. NW, Suite 600
Washington, DC 20005-2164
usta.org

Meet Marty Gorelick

Marty Gorelick has a bachelor of arts degree from Long Island University in New York, along with significant experience in computer hardware sales. He has also attended seminars from all of the major computer manufacturers, such as Compaq, IBM, Hewlett Packard, Sony, Apple, and NEC. He has served as an account manager for a company serving government agencies.

"The computer industry is constantly changing," he says. "It is the fastest-growing industry in the world. Every person on our planet is connected in one way or another. Computers have made communications possible at lightning speed.

"Scientists, doctors, engineers, lawyers, manufacturers, teachers, those in the arts, and every other element of our society operate at higher levels of proficiency than ever before because of computers. For example, a doctor in Seattle can supervise a surgical procedure in an operating room located in Atlanta through the aid of a computer hookup. Ten short years ago, this was impossible. Using a process called computer-aided design, engineers can design structures that will withstand stress far beyond their intended safety limits. Police can track known law offenders well outside of their jurisdiction and notify other law enforcement officers of potential problems. This, by far, is only the tip of the iceberg. Computer applications are endless.

"A typical day for me begins when I arrive at my office about 6:30 A.M. After running the branch's allocation reports for all the salespeople in our office, I check my voice mail for any emergency issues that must be addressed.

An example might be a critical shipment that hasn't arrived on time or a file server that has developed a problem and is inoperable. These situations demand my immediate attention. If both these situations exist, I'll contact our Atlanta facility to run a tracer and our service department to check out the server on their first call of the day.

"I read my E-mail messages next. It's not unusual to have between five and fifteen messages, ranging from company updates to manufacturer price changes to additions and deletions from any number of vendors. Since I give my E-mail address to my customers, I might see a request for a quotation on a product, or clarification of a service agreement, or a question about the configuration of a minitower computer with 256 MB memory, 40 GB hard drive, and a 16X CD-RW drive. Some messages require a response A.S.A.P.; others can be addressed during the course of my regular business day.

"Next stop is my in-mail box, which usually contains a collection of faxes that have arrived since I left the office at the end of business yesterday. These faxes could contain purchase orders, manufacturer promotional notices, seminar information, or news of a prospective customer looking for a great reseller like ours! All this, and the clock has not yet struck 8:00 A.M.

"Now, the doors swing open and my fellow employees arrive. The phones go off night ring and our customers start calling in. We field calls concerning products, service, availability, additions, deletions, and changes in orders.

"During the course of the day, the staff may all assemble for a quick meeting to discuss a change in plans concerning a new company procedure. Our regularly scheduled sales meeting takes place at 8:30 A.M. sharp each Wednesday. This is when we discuss our progress as a group and host a manufacturer who is introducing a new product or products.

"We constantly update our price list to remain the most competitive reseller in the marketplace. I do a special electronic price list for the county every sixty days. This process usually takes me anywhere from three to four working days. I also provide a manuscript of 5,000-plus items from a third-party vendor. On any given day, I may accompany a manufacturer downtown to the county building where we will call on a number of departments that have requested information or a demonstration of a new item.

"Afternoons are generally reserved for cleaning up all unfinished projects, faxing quotes, looking for odd items that appear on purchase orders, and filing away POs and invoices. My day ends about the time that local traffic starts to build on the highway. This represents a ten-plus-hour day, five days a week, four-point-three weeks a month. To say this is a hectic day is putting it mildly. However, if you enjoy what you do, it can be and is a labor of love.

"The most enjoyable part of my position is helping my customers understand their needs with respect to the use of the equipment. An example would be a customer interested in a laptop computer to do presentations at remote sites versus a client needing a laptop for communicating to his home base. One would need a CD-ROM; the other might only need a fax/modem. Some may need both.

"If I had to pick a project I least like to perform, it's the ton of paperwork that is a necessary evil in the day-to-day flow of business. The upside of my business is the satisfaction of being productive and helping others do the same. When I complete a project with confidence in a timely manner so that my customers can enjoy productivity, I take a moment to sit back and breathe easy.

"The downside is always the fact of being in a race with the clock. I try to never let the clock win. I also refuse to let a discontinued product stop me from saying to a customer that I can fill their needs. Somewhere out there is a replacement part. All salespeople are part detective. We look until we find what we need to help our customers.

"For those who are considering entering my world, I would say to be prepared to plan for a very exciting career. Technology advances as fast as you can absorb yesterday's breakthroughs. Pick a school that offers the career path that you wish to follow, sales and marketing, computer network engineering, or service and repair. Attend as many seminars in the field as possible. Read as many journals that pertain to your area of interest as you can. Spend as much time as you can afford talking to those around you in that particular field. Don't be afraid to roll up your sleeves and get your hands dirty. Ask a million questions. Experiment with the knowledge you've gained. Share your findings with others and never stop learning. That's my formula for success."

Meet Jim LeClair

Jim LeClair has gained success as the owner and sales manager for a midwestern computer services company. He earned a high school diploma and took some secondary accounting and business classes. He also has engaged in ongoing seminars and classes that are offered by suppliers to enhance sales, technical training, and product knowledge.

"I was burned out on retail and on working for others," he says, "so my wife and I decided to form our own business. She had a strong computer background and I had more of the business background. We felt our strengths would complement one another. Our company consists of training and network installations—from network design to integration, support, and fiber optics, to name a few.

"We have five employees. Our store hours are Monday through Friday, from 8 A.M. until 5 P.M. The atmosphere is as relaxed as possible, business casual Monday through Thursday, casual on Fridays. Our busiest time of the year is summer.

"I try to keep politics out of the workplace and am flexible with my employees and their families as much as possible. Overtime, for instance, is kept to a minimum.

"A day can change within the first five minutes you walk in the door. You have to be able to juggle things around to grease the squeakiest wheel. I generally arrive at 7:00 A.M. and leave between 6:30 and 7:00 P.M., spending approximately 30 percent of my time administering to the customers' needs, 40 percent working on sales, and 30 percent on day-to-day activities of running the business.

"What I like best is seeing how happy the customer is when we say this is how the network will work and then the network performs as well or better than we anticipated. What I like least is having to discipline employees or contemplate lost sales.

"To be successful in this kind of work, it's very important to keep abreast of the current technology at all times, to be a good listener, to be flexible, to be able to read people, and to understand what they really want, not what they say they want. You have to be able to think quickly on your feet and have a semi-aggressive nature. You just can't take no for an answer. Still, you must sell the customers what they want. Don't try to sell people something that isn't right for them just because you can make some money.

"I'd advise those who are considering computer sales to be honest, to be fair, and to always do a good job. Our business has grown because we have gained the trust of both our customers and our employees."

Path 6:
Other Computer
Science Careers

A large number of careers are open to computer science majors. Even though many of them have been discussed in this book in detail, a number have not been covered due to lack of space. They include account executive at an advertising agency specializing in technology accounts, animation development coordinator, CD-ROM producer, computer book author, computer corporation media spokesperson, computer game animator, computer products project manager, computer trade magazine reporter, cyber cafe owner, cyberlibrarian, director of online service for nonprofit groups, freenet director, Internet access provider, Internet and World Wide Web page designer, multimedia producer, university computer operations coordinator, and virtual reality developer. And this list is not all-inclusive—the opportunities that computer science majors may explore are vast.

Computer Science Professor

Large universities generally direct computer science professors to divide their time between research and teaching. Typically, that equates to teaching two classes a semester, complete with laboratories and office hours, and spending the rest of the week working on ongoing research projects. Professors often teach a lower-level class, such as computer programming, and a graduate-level course, such as advanced software design.

Help Wanted: Computer Science Professor. University teaching professional with experience in teaching computer science or related courses. Ph.D. and research experience required. Fall semester. Local four-year college. Attractive salary and benefits included.

As a professional on staff at a college or university, teachers must attend meetings, grade student papers and projects, mentor students, serve on committees, and attend school functions.

Training and Qualifications

Becoming a professor usually requires a doctoral degree, along with some research and teaching experience. Educators may be assured of continuing employment if they receive tenure (usually available after about six to eight years of teaching and research work at that institution of higher learning). At top computer science departments, attaining tenure is extremely competitive. However, those who fail to become tenured at large universities may be able to achieve this at smaller schools.

Some schools stress research and publication, while others, usually smaller colleges, encourage professors to focus on mentoring students. Many professors cite the satisfaction they receive from teaching the next generation of high-tech pioneers. Other professionals are drawn to academia because of the opportunity it provides to pursue research.

Certain schools, particularly those with computer science departments, look for specialists, such as people who can teach artificial intelligence classes. In other situations, schools seek generalists.

Successful teachers must enjoy teaching and working with students with a variety of different backgrounds and interests.

Earnings

Salaries for assistant professors begin at about $45,000 per year. Tenured professors at large universities can earn $80,000 or more annually. Some universities have department chairpeople who may receive $100,000 or more per year. Not surprisingly, large universities and small elite schools pay more than small state colleges or public community colleges.

Career Outlook

In recent years, securing a position as an instructor at a leading school has become very competitive. Schools have begun to seek professors with specialized skills, such as a Ph.D. with an emphasis in operating systems. However, there are still many opportunities at smaller schools and at state universities.

Professional Associations

American Association of University Professors
1012 Fourteenth St. NW, Suite 500
Washington, DC 20005
aaup.org

Systems Integrators

Systems integrators are responsible for identifying and merging various technologies without disrupting the flow of operations. An example would be merging an inventory control system with a product database to maximize a company's efficiency. Systems integrators also identify weaknesses in current information systems and explore alternative technologies.

Working Conditions

Systems integrators spend most of their time in an office preparing the integration plan. A forty-hour week is standard. Overtime is common as a project nears completion, during installation, or when a design start-up begins. Contract work, perhaps including travel, is not uncommon, usually on a weekly or monthly basis.

Training and Qualifications

Systems integrators need to have a bachelor's degree in computer science, engineering, or information science. Many have master's or doctoral degrees. These professionals are able problem solvers who enjoy analytical thinking. Excellent interpersonal skills and the ability to communicate verbally and in writing are also necessary traits.

Systems integrators often proceed through an apprenticeship and then work their way into an area of specialty.

Earnings

Salaries vary with experience, the location and size of the company, and the responsibilities of the job. Most employers offer paid vacations, holidays, sick leave, and health insurance. The median salary range for systems integrators is about $35,000 to $60,000 per year.

Career Outlook

This is one of the fastest-growing areas in the information technology industry.

Artificial Intelligence Specialist

Artificial intelligence specialists possess a unique and extremely valuable skill—the ability to program computers to imitate the thinking and reasoning processes of the human brain. These professionals have already succeeded in programming computers to do all of the following: make decisions, recognize voices and objects, interpret information, solve problems, and speak in a humanlike voice.

Working Conditions

Artificial intelligence specialists generally work in teams with other experts, usually in research centers. Schedules usually include more than forty hours per week, including evenings and weekends.

Training and Qualifications

These professionals must have a strong background in systems analysis or programming, or fluency in several computer languages. Most have at least a master's degree in computer science or cognitive science, which is an amalgam of psychology, psycholinguistics, computer science, psychology, anthropology, and philosophy. Many have doctoral degrees.

It's also important for artificial intelligence specialists to have patience, dedication, and the ability to work well in a team setting.

Earnings

Earnings vary depending on the setting, location, and specialization of the position. Most employers offer paid vacations, holidays, and health insurance. Trainees in artificial intelligence may earn $25,000 to $45,000 per year. Specialists with a master's degree may earn $45,000 to $80,000 per year. Specialists with doctorates may earn $800,000 to $100,000 per year.

Career Outlook

The field of artificial intelligence is still in its infancy. Job opportunities are expected to grow at a more rapid rate than average, particularly because corporations are very interested in this form of technology. There is ample room for trained, talented newcomers to the field.

Data Entry Keyer

Data entry keyers are sometimes called data entry operators. They enter information into computers where it is stored or used for research purposes.

Working Conditions

Data entry keyers usually work in offices. Since work hours may be long, these workers are susceptible to eyestrain from looking at video display terminals for extended periods. Back strain and carpal tunnel syndrome are also possible.

Training and Qualifications

As a minimum, a high school diploma is required. Data operators must have the ability to enter data accurately at a specified speed. Employers often offer on-the-job training.

Earnings

Salaries may vary considerably depending on the type of company and its location. Typical salaries for data keyers are from $20,000 to $29,500 per year. Some experienced data keyers may earn more than $35,000 per year. Data keyers working for the federal government earn median annual salaries of about $27,000 per year.

Career Outlook

The demand for data keyers is declining, although they will still be needed through 2010. However, opportunities are limited.

Technical Writer (Computer Software Documentation Writer)

The Society for Technical Communication describes technical communicators as serving as "the bridge between those who create ideas and those who use them." With the wide proliferation of sophisticated products now available to consumers, easy-to-understand instructions are needed to explain how to operate such equipment. These instructions are written by technical writers.

Technical writers perform research and then write the instructional guides, reference manuals, and other materials that aid in the use of computer hardware and software. It is their responsibility to make sure that the documen-

Help Wanted. The publications department has openings for senior writers. Candidates should have a bachelor's degree in communications, English, or computer science, strong writing skills, and knowledge of data analysis or closely related software. Visual Basic or related experience also sought. For more information, please send your résumé to Human Resources.

tation is clear enough to help the beginner and detailed enough to be useful to advanced users.

Technical writers must be able to convey the how-to information clearly and concisely. They must organize documents in a logical form and be able to provide good indexes to allow people to find the information they seek. They need skills and experience in graphic design, usability testing (do users really like your work?), programming, publications technology, and project management, as well as good attention to detail.

Possible Job Titles

Information designer	Technical writer
Product communications analyzer	Multimedia writer

Possible Employers

A vast number of industries employ technical writers, including chemical, pharmaceutical, aviation, computer, and electronics businesses. Technical writers may also be employed by research laboratories to write reports on research topics—anything from insect invasion to the search for a cure for diabetes. Federal employers include the U.S. Departments of the Interior, Health and Human Services, Agriculture, the National Aeronautics and Space Administration, and the Department of Defense (which is the largest federal employer). Advertising agencies; newspaper, magazine, and book publishers; professional journals; and colleges and universities also employ technical writers.

Technical writers are also employed by nonscientific members of the community, such as insurance companies, who seek to have their industry's terms and procedures explained. Other possible avenues for employment include composing booklets on employee benefits, writing stockholders' reports, and establishing policies and procedures for any type of operation.

Help Wanted: Technical Writer. Technical writer wanted with a minimum 2 years' technical degree or equivalent experience. Minimum 5 years' technical writing experience in an engineering environment, along with familiarity with the telecommunications industry. Will gather information from engineering resources and product managers to produce/write documentation regarding a variety of highly technical products. Wanted immediately with pay at the market rate.

Related Occupations

A systematic and logical approach is vital to achieve success as a technical writer. Similar skills are necessary for reporters, public relations specialists, and freelance writers.

Working Conditions

Working conditions usually include a pleasant atmosphere in an office containing high-technology equipment. Usually a forty-hour work week is expected. There may, however, be occasional overtime.

Training and Qualifications

Most technical writers earn at least a bachelor's degree, either in technical writing, communications, or English. Some companies require a technical degree with course work in book design and page layout. Writers will be required to produce work that is easily readable and must possess proficiencies in word processing and electronic publishing.

Technical writers usually launch their careers in entry-level positions, frequently as assistants to writers who have already established themselves. Assignments typically include updating copy and proofreading. Novices must become familiar with technical jargon and hone their abilities to confer with scientific and technical experts and translate information into simple terms.

Help Wanted: Technical Writer. Our client has an immediate need for a technical writer to plan, research, and develop documentation, including developer, system manager, and user guides. Must have 3+ years' experience in software technical writing and experience using FrameMaker. Must also have a solid understanding of UNIX, Windows, C/C++, networking principles, and real-time distributed computing.

Pay rate—$45,000 to $65,000 per year.

Research and reporting skills must be sharpened, as well as the ability to write logically, clearly, and precisely.

On a personal level, desirable attributes include excellent communication skills, the ability to meet deadlines and work well under pressure, graphic design abilities, and a good technical understanding of the systems.

Earnings

Some technical writers are paid a weekly salary, while others are paid on an hourly or daily rate. Those who are on staff in a full-time position usually receive vacations, sick days, and other benefits.

According to the U.S. Department of Labor, median annual salaries for technical writers are about $48,000 per year. The middle 50 percent earn between $37,000 and $60,000 yearly. The lowest 10 percent earn less than $24,000, and the highest 10 percent are paid more than $74,000 a year.

Professional Association

Society for Technical Communication, Inc.
901 N. Stuart St., Suite 904
Arlington, VA 22203-1822
stc.org

Tape Librarian

The responsibilities of a tape librarian include classifying and filing the magnetic tapes and disks on which data for computer use are recorded. These professionals also file computer cards and programs, as well as various records such as the operating instructions for computers.

Working Conditions

A typical schedule for tape librarians includes a thirty-five- to forty-hour week in an office, usually near the computer room. There may be some overtime

---

Help Wanted: Library Systems Support Specialist. Our private university is seeking a computer professional to ensure service continuity and support the operations and staff using our state-of-the-art library system.

This position also requires strong service orientation and excellent communication and organizational skills. Associate's degree and computer skills are a must. The selected individual must be able to work flexible hours and weekends.

or shift work if working in large facilities. Tape librarians may spend a great deal of time on their feet while working.

Training and Qualifications

Education and training for tape librarians vary, depending on whether the position is with a library, a data-processing facility, or the government, but at least a high school diploma will be required. In some cases, positions will call for college degrees. People with experience in library work or data processing are preferred. Since each company requires training specific to its particular needs, on-the-job training is generally provided.

Earnings

Salary and benefits for tape librarians vary and are dependent on the size of the library and the type of business or agency. Most positions offer vacations, health insurance, and pension plans. Most tape librarians earn about $18,000 to $30,000 per year.

Professional Association

Special Libraries Association
1700 Eighteenth St. NW
Washington, DC 20009-2514
sla.org

Computer-Aided Design Specialist

Computer-aided design (CAD) specialists are actually designers and drafters who use computers rather than pen and paper to produce their work. Working independently, they may specialize in a variety of tasks.

Working Conditions

CAD specialists spend most of their time in offices working in front of computers. This kind of work over the long term may result in eyestrain and/or fatigue. Usually a forty-hour week is required, but overtime may be required when it becomes necessary to meet deadlines.

Help Wanted: CAD Operator. Manufacturing company seeking experienced CAD operator with HP ME10 or AutoCAD R12 or later. Mechanical drafting experience a plus. Send or fax résumé.

Training and Qualifications

CAD specialists must have expertise in drafting and design. Though this may be taught on the job, most employers require at least a two-year program in drafting and computer technology. CAD specialists must be able to work well with others (especially engineers, designers, and architects); be able to meet deadlines; and have excellent communication skills, both verbal and written.

Earnings

Salaries for CAD specialists vary according to experience and the areas of specialization. Usually, companies offer benefits, including health insurance, pension plans, and paid holidays and vacations. Typical salaries at the entry level range from $25,000 to $35,000 per year, while experienced CAD specialists may earn $40,000 or more per year.

Career Outlook

There is a mixed outlook for CAD specialists. Some say fewer CAD drafters will be needed in the future because computerized systems are becoming easy enough for most engineers, architects, and other designers to use. Others say CAD specialists may be in demand to develop new products. Almost all drafting is now done with the aid of computers.

Computer-Aided Manufacturing (CAM) Technicians

CAM technicians are employed in two different phases of projects. The first is the initial design and setup of the process needed to turn raw materials into finished products. The second is in operating, maintaining, and repairing computer-controlled equipment. CAM technicians assist engineers and designers who develop product designs and specifications, and help to determine the materials needed to make the product and the machines that will be used for its manufacture.

Working Conditions

A good portion of a CAM technician's day is spent in front of a computer. This can be stressful. Sometimes these professionals are required to work evenings or weekends (as there may well be a twenty-four-hour operation at the workplace).

Training and Qualifications

Though a high school diploma is generally the minimum requirement for CAM technicians, most attain at least an associate's degree or complete an apprentice program. Course work should include algebra, geometry, trigonometry, physics, computers, machine shop and electronic training, mechanical drawing, and blueprint reading. Good communication skills and technical expertise are important, along with the ability to identify problems and serve as a troubleshooter.

Earnings

Earnings will vary depending on the size of the company, the type of industry, the geographic location, and the person's level of experience. Generally, benefits such as vacation, holiday pay, health insurance, and pensions are provided by the employer. Most CAM technicians earn between $25,000 and $50,000 per year.

Career Outlook

CAM technicians are needed in one of the fastest-growing areas in the manufacturing industry. CAM technology is increasingly becoming a requirement for manufacturers trying to compete in the international market.

Professional Association

American Design Drafting Association
P.O. Box 11937
Columbia, SC 29211
adda.org

Meet Linda Mikulski

Linda Mikulski earned an associate degree in general studies and an associate's degree in business management, and has served as a lead console operator at a large community college.

"This all happened because I was unemployed due to layoffs in the auto industry," she says. "I was majoring in computer science at Macomb [Illinois] at the time and answered an ad for an entry-level position I was attracted to. The position was in a field entirely different from the one I'd been working in. The monetary rewards were enticing and I enjoyed the atmosphere of the college campus.

"My position is anything but typical," she says. "I operate and program an environmental/ security computer. Not a typical computer job, to be sure. I actually control the air conditioning and heating in all the major buildings on three campuses. I also monitor and control door security and fire security for these buildings.

"A typical day begins with a system check to ascertain what equipment is working and what conditions exist in the buildings. Because I deal with energy conservation, I'm responsible for auditing the amount of gas and electricity our power plants and buildings use. If, for example, electrical demand goes too high (causing us to be penalized by the electric company), my programs must reduce the consumption but must do so without causing undue discomfort to the building occupants. At these times, I must monitor the usage and possibly take steps to override the program, either to reduce consumption or to allow a building to run regardless of the consumption. Because computers allow automated sequencing of building fans (ventilation) without a human being present, part of my job is making sure the computer has the proper information. Special events must be accounted for. Changes in basic scheduling (for instance, we tailor our start-ups and shutdowns with building occupancy, based on classroom usage) must be programmed or checked, and because we monitor fire conditions, part of my daily routine is to ensure the operation of the fire equipment. Conditions are very busy with the beginning of each semester but tend to quiet down after approximately four to six weeks. One of the things we do is take heating or cooling complaints from our clients.

"While my job isn't dangerous since I control large machinery from a distance (one of our campuses is about ten miles from my location), employees who maintain the equipment can be endangered if they don't follow the rules and procedures we've developed.

"My workweek is normally thirty-seven and a half hours, but because I'm a supervisor I tend to put in two to three hours extra each week. The atmosphere at the college is generally relaxed and friendly.

"We tend to upgrade our equipment every four to five years or make additions to the equipment. With the computer industry changing nearly overnight, I have to learn a new system or a new method of controlling the equipment every few years. I feel this keeps the job interesting, and it makes me stretch my mental abilities and awareness. I can't imagine doing the exact same thing for twenty years.

"On the other hand, some of the work can be fairly tedious, no-brainer type stuff. This is along the lines of data gathering and entry, most of which must be done by hand.

"Though the opportunities for advancement are limited, I am heartened by the fact that job security and benefits are very good. Among nonmanagement levels, my position is the highest. Lateral moves into the business end of computer operations are pretty much nonexistent. The type of programming we do is similar to business applications but has more specialized functions. Our department is small, myself and two operators. We cover three shifts per day but only five days a week. We actually work for plant operations (maintenance but not custodial functions). However, we've been located in campus police because of the security aspects of the job.

"Though the emphasis of my job is on computer operation, I'd recommend basic climate-control classes, math, and science to accompany the core computer classes. I've taken all of these at one time or another and found them very helpful in improving my job performance and understanding. I've trained several groups of people not just for Macomb but for Ford Motor Company and for Detroit's People Mover. Those with knowledge of heating and cooling were the first to grasp the principals involved, though they needed more training on computers. Those with only computer experience seem to have a more difficult time assimilating the information provided by the program and therefore a more difficult time in arriving at the correct course of action."

Meet Chris Santilli

Originally a full-time company technical writer, Chris Santilli now spends her time as a freelance technical writer. She earned a bachelor's degree in journalism from Northern Illinois University and a master's degree in journalism from Syracuse University.

"When you're a full-time company technical writer, you're usually working in one industry, so you become an expert in one area," she says. "If you're writing for a medical equipment maker, for example, you become an expert on medical equipment. However, you become more of a generalist if you're given a variety of things to write: technical specifications, features, instruction manuals, instructor notes, and so on. As a freelancer, you may also get a variety of assignments. One day you might be writing about software, the next day you might be writing a procedure manual for a store that sells tires.

"As a freelancer or a company employee, you approach projects in pretty much the same way. You begin by meeting with the product expert—most likely a software, manufacturing, mechanical, or electrical engineer. Sometimes the product you're dealing with is one that's not on the market yet;

sometimes it's not even finished yet. It is likely that this person doesn't speak English as clearly as you do, not that he or she is illiterate by any means. He or she just isn't able to communicate his or her ideas to the layperson. So you have to translate the 'engineer-ese' into more simple language. This means that you have to understand and know how to decipher the lingo. And you must keep in close touch with the expert to be sure that you are saying what he or she intended you to say.

"I work on a project for anywhere from about five or six days, up to six or seven weeks. I usually don't have projects that last six months, but many technical writers do. If you're going to write a software manual for Word-Perfect, for instance, that's going to take a long time and involve many people. I usually work on projects alone or with one other person, so they normally don't take more than two months.

"Most people hear the phrase 'technical writing' and think of computer manuals. But in reality, you could be working for any place that creates any piece of equipment that needs to have something written about it, either how it works, what its specifications are, anything that needs documentation or details a procedure.

"When you are fiddling with a product, you sometimes uncover mistakes. Then you go back to the engineer and say, 'Aha, a little something needs to be fixed here.' It's very personally satisfying to find something like that.

"As a freelancer, you spend a lot of time working by yourself. Very seldom do you have contact with marketing people, but occasionally when you do you might feel slightly frustrated with their use of adjectives.

"There are many pluses to technical writing. The best part is that you work independently, making your own schedules and deadlines within the framework of the project specifications. Technical writing is very rewarding because, as translator and educator, you are an important, integral member of the team.

"If you'd like to get an idea about what it's like to be a technical writer, here's some good advice. Choose an activity such as starting your car, and sit down and try to explain how to do it in a step-by-step process. Begin the explanation from a point right at your front door. 'Step down the stairs, walk across the patio . . .' Remember, nothing can be left out: you must mention every detail. A technical writer needs to be obsessed with detail and accuracy.

"You really have to find pleasure in this kind of work to be successful at it," she says. "Believe it or not, during the summer you'll find me at the beach reading style books just for the fun of it!"

Appendix

Colleges and Universities with Computer Science Programs

The following is a partial list of colleges and universities that offer programs in computer science. Currently, there are more than 1,100 four-year colleges and universities that offer courses of study in the computer field.

Alabama
Alabama A&M University
Normal, AL 35762

Alabama State University
Montgomery, AL 36104

Auburn University
Auburn, AL 36849

Birmingham-Southern College
Birmingham, AL 35254

Central Alabama College
Alexander City, AL 35010

Chattahoochee Valley Community College
Phoenix City, AL 36869

Gadsden State Community College
Gadsden, AL 35902

Huntingdon College
Montgomery, AL 36106

Jacksonville State University
Jacksonville, AL 36265

Samford University
Birmingham, AL 35229

Spring Hill College
Mobile, AL 36608

Stillman College
Tuscaloosa, AL 35403

University of Alabama
Tuscaloosa, AL 35487

University of Mobile
Mobile, AL 36613

University of North Alabama
Florence, AL 35632

University of South Alabama
Mobile, AL 36688

Alaska
University of Alaska, Anchorage
Anchorage, AK 99508

University of Alaska, Fairbanks
Fairbanks, AK 99775

Arizona
Arizona State University
Tempe, AZ 85287

Central Arizona College
Coolidge, AZ 85228

Northern Arizona University
Flagstaff, AZ 86011

University of Arizona
Tucson, AZ 85721

Arkansas
Arkansas State University
State University, AR 72467

Harding University
Searcy, AR 72149

Henderson State University
Arkadelphia, AR 71999

University of Arkansas
Fayetteville, AR 72701

California
California Institute of Technology
Pasadena, CA 91125

California State University
Los Angeles, CA 90032

National University
La Jolla, CA 92037

Pepperdine University
Malibu, CA 90265

Stanford University
Stanford, CA 94305

University of California
Berkeley, CA 94720

University of California, San Diego
La Jolla, CA 92093

Whittier College
Whittier, CA 90608

Colorado
Colorado State University
Fort Collins, CO 80523

National Technological University
Fort Collins, CO 80626

University of Colorado
Denver, CO 80217

Connecticut
Central Connecticut State University
New Britain, CT 06050

Fairfield University
Fairfield, CT 06430

Southern Connecticut State University
New Haven, CT 06515

University of Connecticut
Storrs, CT 06269

University of Hartford
West Hartford, CT 06117

Yale University
New Haven, CT 06520

Delaware
Delaware State University
Dover, DE 19901

University of Delaware
Newark, DE 19716

District of Columbia
American University
Washington, DC 20016

Georgetown University
Washington, DC 20107

University of the District of Columbia
Washington, DC 20008

Florida
Daytona Beach Community College
Daytona Beach, FL 32115

Edison Community College
Fort Myers, FL 33906

Florida State University
Tallahassee, FL 32306

University of Central Florida
Orlando, FL 32816

University of Miami
Coral Gables, FL 33124

University of Tampa
Tampa, FL 33606

Georgia
Albany State University
Albany, GA 31705

Emory University
Atlanta, GA 30322

Gainesville College
Gainesville, GA 35003

Georgia Institute of Technology
Atlanta, GA 30332

University of Georgia
Athens, GA 30602

Hawaii
University of Hawaii
Hilo, HI 96720

Idaho
Boise State University
Boise, ID 83725

University of Idaho
Moscow, ID 83844

Illinois
Bradley University
Peoria, IL 61625

DePaul University
Chicago, IL 60604

Illinois Institute of Technology
Chicago, IL 60616

Knox College
Galesburg, IL 61401

Northeastern Illinois University
Chicago, IL 60625

Northern Illinois University
DeKalb, IL 60115

Northwestern University
Evanston, IL 60208

Roosevelt University
Chicago, IL 60605

Southern Illinois University
Carbondale, IL 62901

University of Illinois
Urbana–Champaign, IL 61820

University of Illinois at Chicago
Chicago, IL 60607

Indiana
Indiana State University
Terre Haute, IN 47809

University of Evansville
Evansville, IN 47722

Valparaiso University
Valparaiso, IN 46383

Iowa
Drake University
Des Moines, IA 50311

Grinnell College
Grinnell, IA 50112

University of Dubuque
Dubuque, IA 52001

Kansas
Kansas State University
Manhattan, KS 66506

University of Kansas
Lawrence, KS 66045

Kentucky
Kentucky State University
Frankfort, KY 40601

University of Kentucky
Lexington, KY 40506

University of Louisville
Louisville, KY 40292

Louisiana
Louisiana State University
Shreveport, LA 71115

Tulane University
New Orleans, LA 70118

Maryland
College of Notre Dame of Maryland
Baltimore, MD 21210

U.S. Naval Academy
Annapolis, MD 21402

Massachusetts
Boston College
Chestnut Hill, MA 02467

Harvard University
Cambridge, MA 02138

Michigan
University of Michigan
Ann Arbor, MI 48109

Wayne State University
Detroit, MI 48202

Minnesota
Concordia College
Moorhead, MN 56562

University of Minnesota
Duluth, MN 55812

Mississippi
University of Mississippi
University, MS 38677

Missouri
Missouri Southern State
College
Joplin, MO 64801

Montana
Montana State University
Bozeman, MT 59717

Nebraska
Peru State College
Peru, NE 68421

Nevada
University of Nevada
Las Vegas, NV 89154

New Hampshire
University of
New Hampshire
Durham, NH 03824

New Jersey
Princeton University
Princeton, NJ 08544

New Mexico
College of Santa Fe
Santa Fe, NM 87505

New York
Columbia University
New York, NY 10027

Cornell University
Ithaca, NY 14853

North Carolina
Duke University
Durham, NC 27706

North Dakota
University of North Dakota
Grand Forks, ND 58202

Ohio
Ohio State University
Columbus, OH 43210

Oklahoma
Oklahoma State University
Stillwater, OK 74078

Oregon
Oregon State University
Corvallis, OR 97331

Pennsylvania
University of Pennsylvania
Philadelphia, PA 19104

Virginia
Virginia Tech
Blacksburg, VA 24061

Washington
Washington State University
Pullman, WA 99164

West Virginia
Bethany College
Bethany, WV 26032

West Virginia University
Morgantown, WV 26506

Additional Resources

ACM Computing Surveys
Association for Computing Machinery
One Astor Plaza
1515 Broadway
New York, NY 10036-5701
acm.org

America's Job Bank
ajb.dni.us

BYTE
byte.com

Career Resource Homepage
careerresource.net

Careers for Computer Buffs & Other Technological Types
VGM Career Books

CAREERS & the disABLED

Computer News Daily
computernewsdaily.com

Computerworld
computerworld.com

Datamation
datamation.com

DM Review
dmreview.com

Equal Opportunity Publications, Inc.
445 Broad Hollow Rd., Suite 425
Melville, NY 11747
eop.com

The 50 Best Jobs for the 21st Century (video)
JIST Publishing, Inc.
8902 Otis Ave.
Indianapolis, IN 46216
jistworks.com

Graduate & Professional Programs: An Overview
Peterson's
petersons.com

The Handbook of Private Schools
Porter Sargent Publishers, Inc.
11 Beacon St., Suite 1400
Boston, MA 02108

IEEE Publications
IEEE Computer Society
10662 Los Vaqueros Cir.
P.O. Box 3014
Los Alamitos, CA 90720-1264
computer.org/publications

Index of Majors and Graduate Degrees
The College Board
45 Columbus Ave.
New York, NY 10023
collegeboard.com

Information Week
CMP Media
600 Community Dr.
Manhasset, NY 11030
iweek.com

National Center for Education Statistics
U.S. Department of Education
Office of Educational Research and Improvement
1990 K St. NW
Washington, DC 20006
nces.ed.gov

National Directory of Internships
National Society for Experiential Education
9001 Braddock Rd., Suite 380
Springfield, VA 22151
nsee.org

Network World, Inc.
118 Turnpike Rd.
Southborough, MA 01772
networkworld.com

NetworkMagazine
networkmagazine.com

Occupational Information Network Resource Center
U.S. Department of Labor
Employment and Training Administration
onetcenter.org

Occupational Outlook Handbook
Occupational Outlook Quarterly
U.S. Department of Labor
Bureau of Labor Statistics
Washington, DC 20212
stats.bls.gov/oco/home.htm

Opportunities in Computer Careers
VGM Career Books

PC Magazine
Ziff Davis Media, Inc.
28 E. Twenty-Eighth St.
New York, NY 10016
pcmag.com

Peterson's Education Center
Career Ed/Guidance
petersons.com

Peterson's 4 Year Colleges
Peterson's Guide to Distance Learning Programs
Peterson's 2 Year Colleges
Peterson's Scholarships, Grants & Prizes
Peterson's
Princeton Pike Corporate Center
2000 Lenox Dr.
Princeton, NJ 08648
petersons.com

Praxis Series: Professional Assessments for Beginning Teachers (formerly National Teachers Exam)
Educational Testing Service
Rosedale Rd., Mailstop 50-B
Princeton, NJ 08541
ets.org

Upside Magazine
upside.com

Index